Sports and Games
History and Origins

Brian Jewell

MIDAS BOOKS

In the same illustrated series

Victorians on the Thames	Reginald Bolland
Fairs and Revels	Brian Jewell
Spas and Watering Places	Muriel V. Searle
Port Out, Starboard Home	Anna Sproule
The Working Travellers	Brian Jewell
Bathing Machines and Bloomers	Muriel V. Searle
Nation of Shopkeepers	Brian Jewell (in preparation)
Circuses and Menageries	Brian Jewell (in preparation)

The book is dedicated to my wife Pat, whose help and forbearance over the long lonely periods of research have been invaluable.

I recall with gratitude and affection the time when she was crouching by torchlight over a broadsheet on the Rules of Cockfighting in the Guildhall Museum, Boston, reading into a tape recorder what must have seemed an endless stream of words, while the custodian was waiting anxiously to close the museum.

First published in 1977 by
MIDAS BOOKS
12 Dene Way, Speldhurst,
Tunbridge Wells, Kent TN3 0NX

© Brian Jewell 1977
Designed by John Rickman

ISBN 0 85936 075 X

Printed in Scotland by
John G. Eccles, Inverness

Contents

Cover/Jacket: *Children's Games* by Brueghel

Endpapers: The Interior of the Fleet Prison — The Rackets Court.

Acknowledgements

The author would like to acknowledge the co-operation of many friends and correspondents with whom, over the years, he has had the pleasure of exchanging information.

Special thanks are due to:

Mr E.W. Aubrook, FMA: Mr John Batterbee; Mr Peter J. Bell; Mr Roy Bennett; Mrs P.V.B. Bevan; Mrs K.F. Biggs; Mr F.J. Bird; Mr Norman Bray; Mr C.P. Burney; Mr C. Burton; Mr R.P. Burton; Mr John Carleton; Mr M.L. Charlesworth; Mr Brian E. Coleman; Mr C. Daniel; Mr. N.W. Davies; Mr Ian Dewhirst; Tony and Jennie Dunbar; Mr G.W. French; Mr Bob Friend; Brig. J.R.C. Gammon; T.G. Gibbons; Miss J. Gordon; Mr C. Ivan Gray; Mr Stephen Green; Mr C. Hancock; Mrs M.E. Harper; Major D.H. Harrison; Mr C.E. Henty-Dodd; Mr J.B.T. Hone; Mrs M.E. Hope; Miss Gillian Howe; Mr D. James; Mr J. Jarvis; Mr Les Jones; Miss Dorothy Laird; Mr George R. Lincoln; Mr W.N.B. Loudon; Miss C.M. Lumley; Mr C.A. Macey; Mr A.H. McQueen; Mr R. Malden; Mr H.A. Matthews; Mr R. Matthews; Mr K.E. Meaney; Mr H.H. Mills; Mr E.H. Paine; Miss M.E.J. Moss; Mr Gerald W. Murray; Mr Gilbert Odd; Mr J. Ogden; Mr Manfred Page; Mr D.F. Petch; Mr S.B. Reay; Mr Maurice B. Reckitt; Mr W. Rossiter; Mr H.A.E. Scheele; Mr. H.F.C. Silcock; Mr R.J.W. Struthers; Mr D. Sutton; Miss M. Swan; Mr Anthony Swift; Mr Peter Tierley; Mr Peter Tombling; Mr Derek Tremayne; Mr F.J. Underhill; Mr R.L. Valentine; Mr G. Wanlass; Miss Anne Ward; Mr Ashton Watts; Mr Herbert Wells; Mr R.G. Westphal; Mr E.L. Whittaker; Mr B.E. Willis; Mr A.R.D. Wright, MA.

Appreciation is also due to the following organisations and institutions whose co-operation has been invaluable in verifying historical details: The Society of Archer Antiquaries; The Alnwick Museum; The Alpine Club; The Amateur Athletic Association; The Ashbourne County Secondary School; Atherstone High School; The Auto-Cycle Union; The Badminton Association of Great Britain; The Amateur Basketball Association; The Bishop Lonsdale College of Education; The Boling Museum, Bradford; Boston (Lincolnshire) Public Library; The Bowes Museum, Barnard Castle; The Bolling Hall Museum, Bradford; The British Canoe Union; The British Chess Federation; The British Ice Hockey Association; The British Museum; The British Sub-Aqua Club; The Castle Museum, York; The Corstopitum Museum, Corbridge; The British Cycling Federation; The Debtor's Prison Museum, York; The Edinburgh Academy; The English Table Tennis Association; Gaelic Sport; The Grantham Municipal Museum; The National Greyhound Racing Society of Great Britain Limited; The Grosvenor Museum, Chester; The Guildhall Museum, Boston, Lincolnshire; The Guild of Agricultural Journalists; The Hallerton School; Harrow School; The Hastings Public Library, Museum and Art Gallery; The Haxey Primary School; The Hockey Association; the British Horse Society; The Hospitals' Trust (1940) Limited; The Inverness Public Library and Museum; The Registry Office of the Jockey Club; The British Judo Association; The Borough of Keighley Art Gallery and Museum; The English Lacrosse Union; The Leicester Museums and Art Gallery; The Lawn Tennis Association; The Leas School, Hoylake; The Ludlow Museum; Marlborough College; The Marylebone Cricket Club; Mary Queen of Scots House, Jedburgh; The National Coursing Club; The Norris Museum, St. Ives, Huntingdonshire; The P & O Lines Limited; The City of Perth Art Gallery and Museum; The Racing Information Bureau; The National Rifle Association; The Museum of Roman Antiquities, York; The Royal and Ancient Golf Club of St Andrews; Sedgefield Rural District Council; The Skipton Public Library and Museum: The Squash Rackets Association; Stockton-on-Tees Public Library; Museum and Art Gallery; Messrs Strawson Limited; The Tolson Memorial Museum, Huddersfield; Vauxhall Motors Recreation Club; The British Amateur Weight Lifters' Association; The York Public Library.

Author's Note

In 1801 Joseph Strutt presented *Sports and Pastimes of the People of England,* an invaluable documentation of the sports and games of his own and earlier times. With such example and inspiration I have attempted to summarise most of the competitive recreational activities which have been recorded up to the year 1900.

It has been difficult to condense all the material found during research into a book of manageable size and in consequence protracted descriptions have been avoided, except in cases where the activity has been so lost in obscurity that it would be difficult to find details elsewhere.

Moreover, I have been forced to omit card and board games. Such games played on a table are so large in number that they must be the subject for a separate book.

I have attempted to suggest families of sports and games, each related to the other by some common bond, although it must be admitted that in places the thread wears a little thin.

The dictionary gives the definition of sport as *a field diversion* and that of a game as *a contest of recreation,* but the neatest and most precise explanation I know is by Sir Alfred Lunn who said that the essence of all sport is the invention of an artificial problem and the finding of a solution to it. If one accepts this definition, then the words *sport* and *game* are interchangeable and this is how I have used them in this book, without apologies.

There are light-hearted games, serious games, deadly games, distasteful games, peaceful games, skilful games, brutal games, foolish games — but they are all of the people, and as such are deserving of our attention, admiration, and in some cases, condemnation — although I have tried to refrain from personal comment. Each reader will no doubt form his or her own opinion.

I have enjoyed writing this book with all the contacts and friends it brought me during its research. I am most grateful to the people who have helped me with information and advice — officials of clubs and organisations, curators of museums, librarians, historians, schoolteachers, and people in public houses in various parts of the country. My sincere thanks to them all.

Tunbridge Wells, 1977   B.J.

1. Combat Contests

'My dad can beat your dad', says the little boy to his playmate, and quite openly he would enjoy the sight of his father sending another man sprawling on the pavement. It is fact, if unpleasant, that people gain enjoyment in seeing their favourites show physical superiority over a challenged opponent, and that state of affairs has been with us for a very long time, certainly since the beginning of recorded history.

But what of the contestants? Throughout the ages men have often engaged in barbaric forms of combat. We all know the exhiliration of victory but on the other side of the coin there may be mutilation and often fatal defeat. Was it worth it? And for that matter — for there are still some very hazardous sports in existence — is it worth it today? The participants themselves certainly seem to think that it is, and one can understand the satisfaction in conquering fear up to the time of involvement, the high degree of concentration during the event, and the hope of the sweet taste of victory. The two latter sensations are to be found in most sports and games, even those in which teams are concerned, but in personal combat sports they are sharpened by the element of risk.

Wrestling is the oldest and purest of personal combat sports. Men must have been trying their strength and unarmed skill since the beginning of time. Egyptian murals on the tombs of Beni Hasan, dating back to 3000 BC show wrestlers in combat and we know that this sort of competition was part of the early Olympic Games. In fact it is said to have been introduced at the 18th Olympiad about 704 BC. There were public contests for professional wrestlers at Delphi, Corinth, Nemea and Olympia. The great wrestler, Milo of Croton, was the unbeaten champion in the Olympics and Isthmian Games for many years, and it is said that when he was building up his physique he carried a young calf a certain distance each day so that as the animal grew heavier with advancing age, so Milo's muscles developed.

Wrestling has for long been part of the English sporting pattern; for instance it was customary in London to hold wrestling matches on Lammas Day. Often the tempers of the spectators ran as high as, or even higher, than those of the contestants themselves.

The 1868
Tournament of the
17th Lancers at
Shorncliffe Camp

7

The Cross Buttock

With Cudgel Play, Quarterstaffs and Sword Play, wrestling was one of the main sporting activities at country fairs and revels right up to the 19th century.

It was through the introduction into England of the Graeco-Roman style of wrestling that public interest in the sport declined. Despite its name, this style of wrestling has nothing to do with the classic styles. It is, in fact, an import from France between 1860 and 1870. In Graeco-Roman wrestling, no holds are permitted below the waist and as the holds may continue on the floor, the bouts can be of considerable duration. It is said that matches sometimes lasted up to eleven hours — a tedious performance, even for enthusiastic spectators!

Traditionally wrestling has two main centres in England: in the West Country, where the Devonshire and Cornwall styles were developed, and in the Northern counties, the home of the Cumberland and Westmorland styles.

Abraham Cann in the early 19th century was backed against any man in England for £500, according to William Hone in his *Every-Day Book*. Cann was a wrestler of the Devonshire style. He and others from his county, such as Jordan, were often objected to for 'showing the toe' — kicking. This was an acknowledged method, quite within the rules, in Devon but not in Cornwall, and there were many Cornishmen who would not 'go in' against a Devon opponent. The Devonshire style exponents justified their somewhat brutal methods by explaining that their style was more classic, and that the Greeks themselves used to kick in their bouts.

The Eagle Tavern in the City Road, London, has been immortalised in the children's song *Pop Goes The Weasel,* but this is not its only claim to fame. In the 1820s the public house was a wrestling centre. One writer of the period describes the differences between the men from Devon and Cornwall after visiting The Eagle:

The florid chubby-faced Devon man is all life in the ring, holding himself erect, and offering every advantage to his opponent. The sallow sharp-featured Cornwall man is all caution and resistance, finding himself in such a way, that his legs are inaccessible to his opponents, and waiting for the critical instant when he can spring in upon his impatient adversary.

Cornish style is said to originate from the Celts and, traditionally, it is always held in the open air, and in a ring. The umpires are known as *sticklers* and usually four or six of these officials are appointed.

Ancient Wrestling

Ancient Wrestling

The legs of the wrestlers are bare from the knees and they wear canvas jackets which must be used in the holds. Traditionally the challenge takes the form of throwing a cap in the air, and whoever wants to may pick it up.

The object is to throw one's opponent so that he lands with both hips and one shoulder, or two shoulders and one hip, squarely on the ground.

Illustrating Cornwall's close connection with wrestling was the banner of the Cornish troops in the Hundred Years War, which showed two wrestlers in action.

The other main division of traditional English wrestling is that known as Cumberland and Westmorland style, a form of contest said to have been introduced by the Vikings.

Mr H. A. Matthews, whom I met in Haltwistle, Northumberland, recalled the village green wrestling he took part in as a small boy at the turn of the century. All the competitors' caps were thrown into the air and matches were made depending upon the way the caps fell — those falling next to each other being paired off regardless of weight.

The aim is the 'best of three falls' as it is in most matches of 20th century professional wrestling. The loosening of the opponent's grasp also constitutes a fall, the combatants clasping hands behind each other's back, with the right hand over the opponent's, and chins on each other's shoulders.

One of the giants of Cumberland style wrestling was George Steadman of Whitehaven, who wrestled and won at the Grasmere Sports at the age of 51 years in 1896, having embarked on his wrestling career in 1862.

Kicking seems to have been part of the wrestling scene everywhere except in Cornwall. Shinning or Cutlegs was a recognised sport and even today schoolboys play a variation which they call Stampers — as its name implies, it calls for stamping on each other's toes.

The Hipe

At the Wheatsheaf Inn at Corbridge-on-Tyne, I have been told of a local kicking variation called Kick Bonny White Horse. In this the contestants stand back-to-back with their arms linked, and start kicking away with their heels at each other's calves — much less painful than the front kicking at the bony part of the shin which goes on in Devonshire style wrestling!

Lancashire style wrestling is a form of Catch-as-catch-can which allows considerable freedom of movement and is similar to the free style favoured by followers of modern professional wrestling. It has a reputation of being particularly barbarous, although the rules specifically bar throttling or the breaking of limbs! The contestants start apart and not in holds as in the Cumberland and Westmorland style. There are few restrictions and the holds continue on the ground, which means that the bouts can become very long drawn-out affairs.

There is a quotation on Lancashire style in the Wrestling book of the Badminton Library:

A Lancashire wrestling-match is an ugly sight: the fierce animal passions of the men which mark the struggles of maddened bulls, or wild beasts, the savage yelling of their partisans, the wrangling, and finally the clog business which settles all disputes and knotty points, are simply appalling.

Scottish style wrestling can best be described as a cross between Cumberland and Westmorland style and Catch-as-catch-can, while the other style in the British Isles — Irish Wrestling — involves the contestant taking hold of his opponent's collar with one hand and his elbow with the other.

In Iceland the national style of sporting combat is Glima in which a kind of leather harness is worn around the loins and this is used when making holds. Something similar is performed in Switzerland where, in place of the leather harness, strong canvas trousers are worn in a style of wrestling called Schwingen.

The Indian style of wrestling combat is called Guile. This is a form of combat which calls for a considerable strength and often the bouts are long-lasting in consequence. It is an extremely skilful form of combat involving more than 400 tricks or *penches* which have to be learned before a man can be called a *pulwan* or expert.

Although popularly believed to be of Japanese origin, it is more likely that China was where Jiu Jutsu and Judo began, probably in the pre-Christian era.

The Hank

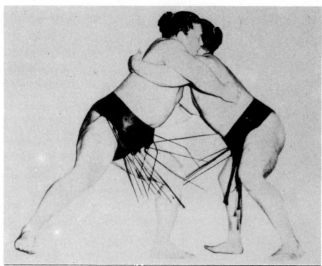

Japanese Sumo
Wrestling

It is said that it was a Chinese priest called Chin Genpin who, in 1659, took Kempo, a form of unarmed combat, to Japan. It was the *serious* combat version of the sport of Judo which depended to a large extent on using the opponent's strength to his disadvantage.

It must be admitted however, that the modern Judo was undoubtedly developed in Japan. Its name literally means the *soft way*. In the early 1900s Dr Jigoro Kano (who developed the art in Japan in 1882) introduced the *artform* to Britain. There were also demonstrations in Music Halls by Yokio Tani and Raku Uyenishi, the latter opening a Judo school in London's Golden Square — quite a breakaway from the old Japanese tradition of confining the secrets of this form of combat to the Samurai caste.

Karate, that formidable and fascinating mysterious sport, probably has, like Jiu Jutsu, its origin in a form of Chinese combat. We do know that it was developed as a means of guerilla fighting by the conquered and disarmed inhabitants of Okinawa in the Ryukya Islands in the 17th century. It became a sport, and to some extent a way of life, as late as 1916. The word *karate* means *open hand* which distinguishes it from the closed fist varieties of unarmed combat. There are six styles of Karate with specialists in each: Shotokan — with emphasis on technique; Kyo-Kushinkai — with more strength involved; Wado-Ryu, Gojo-Ryu, Shito-Ryu — speed versions of the sport; and Kwan-do — the lethal form of Karate which probably has its origins in the Okinawa guerillas.

Unarmed combat has a long history in Japan: Sumo Wrestling is thought to have originated about 2000 years ago and it is said that in the year 23 BC the Emperor matched two strong men, Kehayer and Nomino-Sukano, the former being killed.

Fighting with the fists for sporting motive may well, as some authorities say, have its origins in Greek Mythology.

Although a form of unarmed combat like wrestling, so far as Britain is concerned, it grew up quite separately, more as a replacement for Cudgel Play, to become a serious sporting activity only when the carrying of weapons was going out of fashion.

It was one James Figg (1695-1734) who first brought *pugilism* into prominence in London in 1719, when he became British Champion, a title he kept for eleven years.

Jack Broughton

1740 to 1750 were the great years for Jack Broughton (1704-1789), who must be considered the father of the sport. It was Broughton, under the sponsorship of the Duke of Cumberland, who formulated the first *Rules of Prize Fighting* in 1743, an attempt to bring some order into a sport which, up till then, was virtually nothing more than a brawl. At that time Broughton was running a prize fighting establishment behind Oxford Road in London, near Tottenham Court Road. Under the Broughton Rules fighting had to be contested on a stage — called the *ring* and probably named after the ring used in Cornwall Style Wrestling. This stage was set 6ft above floor level to prevent the patrons climbing in and joining in the fight.

Broughton Rules were quite specific and a considerable advance on the old free-for-all type of fighting previously seen:

That a square of a yard be chalked in the middle of the stage, and every set-to after a fall or being parted at the rails, each second to bring his man to the square and place him opposite to the other, and until they are fairly set-to at the line, it shall not be lawful for the one to strike the other.

That in order to prevent any disputes as to the time a man lies after a fall, if a second does not bring his man to the side of the square within the space of half a minute he shall be deemed a beaten man. [It is believed that sometimes an extra eight seconds' grace was allowed].

That in every main battle no person whatever shall be upon the stage except the principals and the seconds; the same rule to be observed in big battle, except that in the latter Mr Broughton is allowed to be upon the stage to keep decorum and to assist gentlemen in getting to their places, provided always that he does not interfere in the battle. Everyone is to quit the stage as the champions are stripped before the set-to.

That no champion be deemed a beaten man unless he fails coming up to the line in the limited [time]; or that his own second declares

Boxing. Engraving
by Alken

him beaten. No second is allowed to ask his man's adversary any question or advise him to give.

That in big battles the winning man to have two-thirds of the money given, which will be publicly divided on the stage, notwithstanding any private agreement to the contrary.

Other points in the Broughton Rules were that a fighter would be disqualified if he hit his opponent while he was down, and that two referees should be chosen from the spectators.

Fighters used to pickle their hands in soda, hardening them to a similar extent as the exponents of karate in the 20th century.

No gloves were used in those early days but in practising and training for a fight they used to wear a crude from of gloves called *muflers*.

It was indeed a rough tough murderous sport in which any form of attack was permitted, including biting and kicking.

Prize Fighting was not a legal form of sport after 1863 but eyes were closed by the law administrators as well as by the fighters themselves.

13

It was in 1860 that the death knell for Prize Fighting was first heard, when the British Champion Sayers met the American Heenan (the Benicia Boy), at Farnborough, Hampshire.

After two and a half hours of battering, the result of the fight was declared a draw. The crowd went mad, wanting more blood, and indeed they got it — there were many casualties. After that, public opinion started to turn against the fight game. So great was this feeling that under the *Regulations of the Railways Act, 1868,* it was an offence for a railway company to run a special train to a Prize Fight, the penalty being a £200 fine, half of which went to the informer.

But fisticuffs had its supporters in high places, and movements were afoot to keep the noble sport alive. One of these supporters was the Eighth Marquis of Queensberry (1844-1900), a name and title known well in sporting circles — on the turf as well as in the ring. In 1865 the Marquis and John Chambers set about formulating a new set of rules and, two years later, the first bout was fought under the Queensberry Rules. These were more humane and orderly rules, with rounds of fixed duration, and it is basically these rules under which boxing is carried on today.

Even with all the battering he endured, it is interesting to note that Jack Broughton, who was the Champion of England with many fights behind him, died at the ripe old age of 85 years. Another of Broughton's claims to fame is that he was, in his youth, a winner of the Doggatt Coat and Badge — the oldest surviving rowing race held on the River Thames.

Lion and Man Fight

Gladiators in Arena

Boxing's somewhat strange and contradictory sub-title, the *Noble Art of Self Defence* goes back to before the days of popular Prize Fighting. It was Henry VIII who, in 1540, encouraged the foundation of schools where 'playinge with the two hande sworde, the pike, the bastaerd sworde, the dagger, the backsworde, the sworde and buckler, and the staffe and all other weapons appertyninge to the same science' were taught to those requiring such advantages. These schools were administered by the *Maisters of the Noble Science of Defence*.

The rules of boxing, of course, vary in different parts of the world. For instance, Savate is a form of boxing using the feet as well as the fists; it was a style once used in France and currently in countries in the Far East.

The idea of mortal combat with weapons as a spectacle is undoubtedly a very old one. In Rome where gladiatorial combats were frequent events, human beings fought each other or were matched against animals to give delight to the spectators. Life was cheap.

The idea of men fighting for public amusement may have been borrowed by the Romans from Etruria and probably first presented in Rome about the year 265 BC, initially at funerals and then at festivals. It has also been said that gladiatorial combat came to the Roman Games by accident when two brothers, Marcus and Decimus Brutus, on the death of their father, decided to revive an old custom of having a few slaves fight to death over the grave of a dignitary. Soon politicians and others, in search of favour with the masses, were staging fights with gladiators.

The first Roman Games, held in 238 BC, were tame affairs featuring trick riding, performing animals, chariot racing, acrobats and athletic events. But the Romans tired of this sort of entertainment and were soon devising ever-increasingly bloodthirsty spectacles. By Nero's time, millions of people were dependent on the Games for a livelihood and, if by some remote chance, humane feelings had caused the abandonment of the cruelty, the whole economy would have been at risk. The Games eventually came to cost about one-third of the total income of the Empire. The Romans were on an accelerating roller-coaster and the Games could not be ended until Rome had begun to decline.

Suetonius describes an arena fight between two mixed forces of 20 elephants, 500 foot soldiers and 30 horses each. It has been suggested that Caesar may have been experimenting with the use of elephants for the Parthian War which was then being planned. Caesar often used the Games as a testing ground to try out new weapons and military techniques.

It was not only land forces that were pitched against each other in these deliberate conflicts; there were also *Naumachia* — naval battles. The greatest of these was held on the Lago di Fucino near Rome, when Claudius decided to match two navies of 25 ocean-going warships. For sheer numbers we have to look to Dio's *Epitome* in which we are told that when Trajan celebrated the Dacian Triumph in AD 107, the Games lasted for 120 days; 10,000 gladiators fought and 11,000 animals were killed.

In the 1st century AD there were four gladiatorial schools: The Great School; The Gallic School; The Decan School; and The School for Bestarii — fighters of animals. Travelling groups of gladiators were available for hire at the many arenas throughout the Roman Empire; such places as Pompeii, Nimes, Arles, Capua, Paris, Puteoli, Frejus, Chester, Dorchester, Carthage and Verona. There are remains of over seventy such arenas.

The gladiators were either free-born citizens who fought for hire, and who were usually from a poverty class, or captives,

Singlestick

slaves or malefactors. These were the men who, before combat, cried 'Caesar! nos morituri te salutamus'.

The style of gladiatorial combat took several forms, depending upon their dress or method of fighting. The Andabatores fought blind in helmets with no eye holes; the Mirmillons used Gallic weapons of sword and shield; the Retiarii carried a net and three-pronged lance; the Thraces, like the Thracian warriors, used a short sword and round buckler; the Equites fought on horseback. Others were the Dimacherus, the Samnite, and Secutar.

If a gladiator was fortunate enough to live to retirement he was discharged by being presented with a *Rudis* — a wooden sword. Normally a gladiator had to serve for a period of three years but the crowd, at any time, when greatly impressed by a gladiator's skill or courage, could demand that he be presented with the Rudis at that moment. Sometimes the wooden sword was not accepted; Flamma, one of the most famous gladiators of all time, refused the Rudis on no less than four occasions.

One of the nastiest tasks in the arena was that of the *Confector* who went around despatching the wounded men

17

Backsword

and animals. Carnage was everywhere and medical men used to attend the Games in order to study anatomy.

Somewhat less lethal but still brutal and distasteful to our feelings today — when humane conduct is taught if not always performed — were Cudgal-play, Quarterstaffs, Backswording, and Singlesticks events fought at fairs and revels until the middle part of the 19th century.

The Quarterstaff was a strong iron-tipped pole about 8ft long and about 1½in. in diameter. Originally it was a weapon of attack and defence of English peasants, and features strongly in the stories of Robin Hood and his men. The quarterstaff bore the same relationship to the singlestick as the two-handed sword did to the ordinary sword. As a weapon the Quarterstaff fell out of favour about the time of Charles II.

One version of the quarterstaff play was performed on a narrow plank over a stream, the idea being to push rather than to knock one's opponent into the water. This presumably is the derivation of the Pillow Fight still seen at village fetes in which the contestants sit astride a horizontal pole and attempt to knock each other from their perch.

The singlestick was to be found all over Europe in the 15th century. Lowly people were not permitted to carry swords and

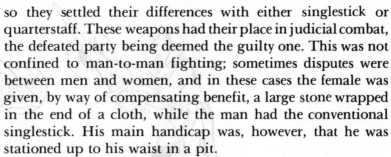

so they settled their differences with either singlestick or quarterstaff. These weapons had their place in judicial combat, the defeated party being deemed the guilty one. This was not confined to man-to-man fighting; sometimes disputes were between men and women, and in these cases the female was given, by way of compensating benefit, a large stone wrapped in the end of a cloth, while the man had the conventional singlestick. His main handicap was, however, that he was stationed up to his waist in a pit.

The Singlestick — a cudgel for use with one hand — was about 3ft long and about 1½ins in diameter. The basketwork hilt to protect the sword hand was introduced about the middle of the 17th century.

The Backsword was demonstrated by prize players from the time of Charles I and possibly earlier. The Purton Fair, in Wiltshire, featured backswording. Traditionally it was a match between four Purton men and four men from Stretten. The losing team had to pay all expenses for the day, including the liquid refreshment! The custom of this fight was discontinued in 1824.

From the *Reading Mercury* of 24 May 1819, we read,

The Peppard Revel will be held on Whit Monday the 31st May 1819; and for the encouragement of young and old gamesters, there will be a good hat to be played for at cudgels; for the first seven couple that play, the man that breaks the most heads to have the prize; and one shilling and six pence will be given to each man that breaks a head, and one shilling to each man that has his head broke.

Time Thrust in Sixte

19

Sword Play

A kind of fencing as a sport is thought to have existed in Egypt as early as the 18th century BC, no doubt as an exercise for the more serious activity of combat in battle; there is a wall painting in a temple at Luxor which depicts two fencers who appear to be wearing masks and using blunted swords.

According to historian Egerton Castle, the form of fencing we now know as a sport became accepted and practical when armour fell into disuse. Before that, the need in sword fighting was more for strength than for great skill. Fencing was a development of the sword and buckler form of combat in which the men did not use armour to protect themselves, the sole defence being the shielding with the buckler.

In 1595 a book on fencing by Vincentio Saviolo was published in London; he, with other fencing masters, had come to this country from Italy. This gentleman is also mentioned by George Silver in his *Paradoxe of Defence* (1599), together with two other 'teachers of offence' in London at that time; Signor Rocko and his son Jeronymo. It is reported that Rocko received between £20 and £100 for a course of instruction.

In England about this time, two styles of fencing were used: the Italian and the Spanish methods. They employed the Long

Buckler Play

Saxon Archers

Saxon Bow and
Arrow

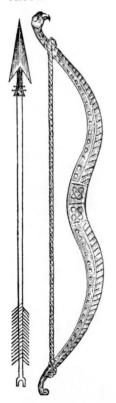

Tuck or the Rapier with very long narrow blades, often double-edged. In time the Rapier was shortened to less cumbersome proportions and became known as the *small sword*. Both the Italians and the Spanish had schools of rapier practice of high repute.

Other weapons were introduced at later periods: the *fleuret* (foil) from France in the 17th century when that country was supreme in the art — the *Academie d'Armes de Paris,* by the way, had been formed in the 16th century — the *Sabre* from Hungary in the 18th century, and the *épée* from Italy as late as the 19th century.

Shooting, whether it be behind a long bow, or through the sights of a rifle, is one of the most individual sports of all. It is also the most warlike, and has been encouraged throughout the ages, from time to time, when archers were a formidable force.

As suggested by General Pitt Rivers, the invention of the bow and arrow may have been inspired by primitive spring traps used to capture animals in forests. Whatever the origin, ancient wall paintings show that bows and arrows were used as hunting weapons at least 20,000 years ago.

The Scythians, Egyptians, Parthians and Thracians were all peoples who used the bow and, at the time of the might of Rome, it was employed by the Cretans, Numidians, and Balearic Islanders, all of whom served as mercenaries with the Roman Legions.

In Britain, shooting as a sport is thought to have become recognised only in the 4th century AD. The words *shaft, bow,* and *arrow* are all of Saxon origin.

21

Practising with the
Cross Bow

The use of the Long Bow was encouraged by Edward I and
the English Archery laws compelled all able-bodied men under
a certain rank to practise with the bow on Sundays and holidays
from childhood up to the age of 60 years. Butts had to be set up
in all villages.

In 1285 there was a Statute of Westminster which forced every
man with an income from land of under 100 pence to possess
bows and arrows. This was followed in 1466 by an Act which
exempted only judges and clerics from keeping the long bow.

The long bow has stood the English in good stead, and the
respect for the weapon is typified by the law as it stood at the
time of Henry VIII, under which the use of hand guns and
crossbows was forbidden as it detracted from practise with the
long bow. Every possible occasion was used to encourage
archery, and it was a regular feature at Tudor fairs. James I

Crossbow Shooting
at the Butts

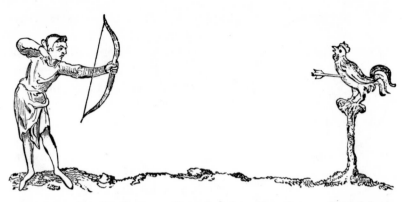

encouraged archery as well as dancing, leaping and vaulting.
These activities were beginning to be considered more healthy
than attendance at animal baiting.

It was in 1673 that the first Scorton Arrow meeting was held
in Yorkshire; this was three years before the Royal Company of
Archers, the Sovereign's bodyguard in Scotland, was formed.
This company, also known as the Royal Scottish Archers, have
in their possession the famous Flodden bow which requires a
pull of between 80 and 90lbs to draw the string.

The group of archers known as the Woodmen of Arden have
kept records since the year 1785. Their headquarters are at
Meridan, Warwickshire, the spot which is traditionally
considered to be the centre of England. The membership of the
Woodmen is limited to 80 in number, under their Perpetual
Warden, the Earl of Aylesford. During the months of June,
July, and August the Woodmen hold their Wardmotes, the
name given to the competitions, culminating in the Grand
Wardmote in the first week in August. These are very colourful
events with Woodmen attired in green coats with silver buttons,
buff waistcoats and white trousers. The weapon used is the 6ft
long bow, England's strength at Crecy and Agincourt.

Before the acceptance of the now universal target with the
gold centre, stuffed or tethered birds were used, particularly in
that division of archery known as Papeguay, Papegai, or
Papegaut. This probably had its roots in the ancient French
custom of *La Bravade de St Jean d'Aix*, which was instituted on
the return of Louis IX's army from the crusades in 1272. The
ceremony was held on the eve of the Feast of St John the Baptist
and involved a large bird tethered in a field so that it had only
limited freedom of flight. When all was set and the bird was
flapping around, 'the sons of the second order of nobles' shot
their arrows at the unfortunate creature and the killer was
appointed King of the Archers for the coming year — a position
that carried considerable benefits. The custom continued until

23

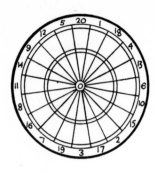

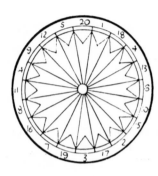

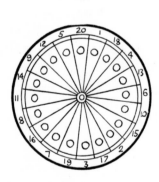

Standard Board
Tonbridge Board
Disc Treble Board

the Revolution and in its latter years a wooden bird on a pole was used in place of a live target.

Papeguay was later anglicised into Popingay or Popinjay.

Popinjay shooting was carried on in the late 19th and early 20th centuries with a target being lifted aloft by a kite.

The Crossbow or Arbalest was probably an invention of The East and was known in the Roman Empire in the 6th century. By the 12th century it was extensively used as a weapon of war. It was, however, a somewhat cumbersome weapon and one that was never really popular in sport.

We must consider Darts as a derivative of archery and it was certainly played a long time before the modern dart board was developed in the latter part of the 19th century.

Edward III prohibited the throwing of stones, darts and arrows in sports and games so that practise with the long bow might be encouraged. We can safely assume, therefore, that some form of hand dart was known then as a means of sport. This was probably similar to those used by archers in close-quarter fighting, and these 10ins missiles might well have been the direct ancestors of those found in almost every pub in the 20th century.

We are told by a number of historians that archers used the ends of wine butts as targets, which seems a good reason why we have round targets instead of square or human-shaped.

Darts are thought to have been played in Ireland in the 16th century and it is also believed they were played on the *Mayflower* in 1630. It is, therefore, surprising that Joseph Strutt does not mention darts in his *Sports and Pastimes of the People of England* published in 1801. The earliest boards had concentric rings only — rather like the modern archery target — and this style of board is still used in Scandanavian countries, the darts themselves being about 1ft long, reminiscent of the hand arrows of centuries ago.

Arrow Pitching (*Pyrkyng or Prycking*), as distinct from dart throwing, was specifically mentioned in an ordinance made by the Corporation of Leicester in 1467, which forbade this and other games on pain of imprisonment.

In Yorkshire the sport of arrow throwing was once very strong. The author has been told by elderly gentlemen of Malton how they used to throw arrows — full sized. These were hurled with the aid of a cord wound around the shaft which caused the arrow to spin in flight so that greater distances could be achieved. The nature of the sport was more like that of throwing the javelin in that it was distance, and not the aiming at targets, which scored points.

24

This method of throwing arrows, spears and javelins by the aid of a cord is a classic one. It was used by the New Caledonians in Captain Cook's time. Even in the days of Rome's glory, the warriors used the *amentum* — a thong which aided the throwing of missiles.

In the latter part of the 19th century the game of darts was more a popular children's game than one for adults in public houses. There was one dart and board game called Dartelle which was successfully sold commercially. About the same time there was also a game called Puff and Dart, in which the latter was blown through a tube at the target, in the same way as the Malay people use the Sumpitan. I believe this game found its way into some taverns to be tried as an alternative to the conventional form of darts.

Musket shooting started to gain ground from hawking and falconry in the 17th century as the standards of firearms and their reliability improved. In 1777, in Ealing High Street, the Old Hat Club was formed to cater for the needs of those who wanted to indulge in the sport of Pigeon Shooting. The members used to meet at various places around London, such as Ealing, Islington, North Cheam and Battersea, where a great amount of money was gambled on the prowess of individual sportsmen. That great man of all sport, Squire George Osbaldestone, whose name appears several times in this book, was a member of the Old Hat and won the Crunden Annual Gold Medal at the sport in 1826.

Blue Rock Pigeons, or farmers' semi-wild pigeons, were the targets. After being shot, the dead bird had to fall within a fenced area in order to score, specially constructed traps having been used to release the birds to their fate. Contests took the form of 100 shots each, the winner being the gun with the best bag, firing at a range of between 30 and 40yds.

Considerable cruelty was involved in the sport, and sometimes the birds were blinded so they would flutter around when released. But the situation was tolerated by the public for many years, in fact until 1921, when a lengthy campaign in *The Times* resulted in the passing of the Captive Birds Shooting (Prohibition) Act. However, live pigeon shooting was still available to the English sportsman abroad. It continued for years on the lawn in front of the Casino at Monte Carlo with birds being released from baskets.

Because of the decline in popularity of captive pigeon shooting in Britain, sportsmen turned to the shooting of clay discs and, in 1893, the Inanimate Bird Shooting Association was formed, a body renamed the Clay Bird Shooting Association in 1903.

In the constitution of the United States of America was written the right of every man to carry arms, a right jealously guarded even at the expense of killing off Presidents by madmen, as we well know.

If it is thought that Americans are gun-crazy today it is advisable to look at their activities of the 18th and 19th centuries when the gun was law in some places, and the sharpest shooter the king. There existed such sporting activities as Shooting at a Tin Mug on a Man's Head at 40 paces — shades of the saga of William Tell — driving a Nail into a Tree, and Shooting at a Lighted Candle, in which the object was sometimes to clip the wick without actually extinguishing the flame.

Fixed Quintain. 14th century

The Saracen Quintain

Tournaments were the old war games in which the Sovereign's knights and their soldiers could practise the warlike arts. The actions were between individuals or whole private armies and were realistic to the extreme, often resulting in fatalities. For example, in 1249 at a Tournament at Neuss, near Cologne, sixty knights were killed in a mêlée.

Tournaments were always discouraged by the Church and, at certain periods, by the State; they were actually forbidden until the reign of Stephen, and were not given any real State support until Richard I gave the warlike games his blessing; but always

Moveable Quintain

26

they had been encouraged in France. Jousting was a different matter. This was the form of combat between two individuals and not quite so barbaric. Indeed, every Royal Palace had its tilt yard.

Jousts were held either as a separate event or as a feature of a Tournament and took two forms: *Joute à Plaisance* in which blunted weapons were used, or the *Joute à l'outrance* (the term used for the ultimate Roman Gladiatorial contest), which was the real thing, with genuine war-sharp weapons.

Jousting was carried out in a large enclosed space, in which the riders, fully armed, rode straight at each other. This became modified to *Tilting* with the contestants riding alongside and either side of a rope, later a wooden fence (or *Toile*) of about 5 or 6ft.

Living Quintain, 14th century

Tilting at the Ring

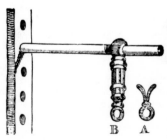

The Ring in Tilting

The Tournament in its early form died out in Tudor times as people were beginning to think that the social activities of merry-making and dancing were to be preferred to the killing and maiming of the old times. It is said by some authorities that it was the death of Henry II of France in a tournament in 1559 that led to the abandonment of the more dangerous aspects in that country.

But to get back to basics, the Tournament, as we think of it has been ascribed by some authorities to Emperor Henry the Fowler who died in the year 936, while others think it was the invention of Geoffry de Preuilly who died in 1066.

27

Preparation for a Tournament

Toy Quintain

Henry VIII tried to revive the Tournament in its tougher form but despite his efforts the affairs softened and refinements were introduced, such as straw on the falls when Jousting, much to the disgust of the public.

The word *Carousel* has been used to describe Running At The Ring but originally it took its name from *Carosello*, a game in which was used a hollow ball of chalk about the size of an apple. The party divided themselves into two teams who rode at each other hurling the balls as they went. It was played extensively in Spain where it was called *Alcancias*. Sometimes light canes were used in place of the chalk balls, when the sport was called the *Feste di Cannas*.

Tilting at, or Running at The Ring became popular in Henry VIII's reign. It had been introduced about 200 years earlier but had not been considered adventurous, or perhaps bloodthirsty, enough. It consisted merely of a ring suspended from a pole, past which the contestant galloped trying to impale the ring with his lance.

Riding at the Quintain was a kind of tilting using a machine which could hit back. The machine consisted of a target on a beam at the other end of which was suspended a sack of sand or stones. The beam pivoted horizontally at its centre on an upright pole. Sometimes the target was a wooden figure to represent a Saracen but more often it was just a wooden board. The idea was to gallop past, hit the target and get out of the way fast enough to prevent the sack of stones coming around and knocking the contestant from his horse.

J. Stowe in *Survey of London* (1631) wrote that he saw a Quintain set up at Cornhill, near Leadenhall, where it was well attended. Since Tudor times, it had become the poor man's tournament type of pastime, whereas in earlier days the tilting games were the right only of those above the rank of knight.

Jousting, 14th century

The Mêlée, 15th century

Quintains were also played on foot and over water.

The quintain over the years has taken many forms — some had a barrel of water on a beam pivoted vertically instead of horizontally. This sort of quintain can still be seen at some village summer fetes. Often village greens had their own permanent quintain and an example of such has survived the years at the village of Offham in Kent, standing proudly on the green.

Children have often used the quintain idea in play, substituting for the bag of stones a bag of feathers and using sticks with horses' heads instead of real horses. A charming toy of the 19th century and possibly earlier was the Miniature Quintain which consisted of a carved wooden model of the upper part of a Saracen's body, with a shield in one hand and a sword in the other. The whole toy stood only about 4ins high and was so delicately balanced that it could swing around. The object was to give the shield a push and withdraw the finger before the sword came round to hit it.

Another event held at Tournaments was the Baston Course which originated in the 15th century. It is a form of combat with two contestants on foot. Between them is a low wall — about 5ft high — the outcome of the tilting wall used to protect

30

the horses and to stop the combatants riding headfirst into each other. The Baston Course opponents wore heavy padded helmets with an emblem on the top. They also carried a club each. The object of the game was to smash the other man's emblem and to avoid the blows of his club by ducking.

Yet another form of tilting was with the contestants mounted on stilts — going back to the time when stilts were used for scaling high walls in battle.

A few of the Tournament events survived in military sports, at least as long as the cavalry was the most important part of the army. There were such regimentally recognised events as the *Balaclava Mêlée* in which teams of four or six men on horseback, wearing padded jackets and helmets adorned with paper plumes, tried to knock off each other's plumes. Tilting at the Ring continued as an event in military sports until the end of the 19th century, as did the allied sports of Ball and Bucket, Lemon Cutting, Heads and Posts, and Tent Pegging.

Ball and Bucket, as its name suggests involved the dropping of a ball into a bucket while galloping past. Lemon Cutting belonged to a similar family of games, with the lemons suspended at shoulder height to be cut with a heavy sword or *lead cutter*.

Heads and Posts was a game that needed the same kind of action as Lemon Cutting, in which dummy heads were bobbed up and down behind screens. The contestants had to gallop past and decapitate the figures. Tent Pegging had something of a mixture of Tilting at the Ring and the Indian sport of Pig Sticking. In Tent Pegging the competitors galloped past the pegs and tried to remove them with a lance.

Mêlée type combats have had their place in military sports using dummy rifles with wooden bayonets that would slide up the barrel, and singlesticks instead of swords.

The raising of heavy weights by strong men was one of the attractions of the country fairs and revels, but these were purely exhibitions of strength and not events of a competitive nature.

Although there was considerable interest in weight-lifting feats during the 18th century, particularly in America, the sport as we know it in its organised form is of fairly modern origin, the first world championship taking place at the Cafe Monico, in London's Piccadilly in 1891.

It is uncertain when and where Tug of War began; it is recorded that in 1889 there was a regimental contest at Jubblepore, India, but we can trace the idea a good deal further back than that date. W. Felton in *A New Guide to the Town of Ludlow,* (1822) records an annual Shrove Tuesday event at

Ludlow called Pulling a Rope. A rope, 3ins thick and about 36yds in length, provided by the Chamberlain or Chief Constable, was passed out of a window in the Market Hall as 4 o'clock in the afternoon was struck.

The town had divided itself into two teams and, although no numbers in each team were specified, the weights seemed to work out fairly equally, the teams comprising the Castle Street and Broad Street wards on one side, and the Old Street and Corve Street wards on the other. It is said by William Hone in the *Every-Day Book* (1827) that in 1826 some 2,000 people took part. As many men as possible caught hold of the rope and commenced to pull. When one side had pulled the opposing team over a prescribed distance, the losers purchased the rope from the victors for £2 to £3 and the pulling was repeated. At the end of the day the money so gained was spent on ale for the evening's merry-making.

Felton writes, 'The Corporation do not avow the motive for continuing this uncouth practice'. However, Hone submits that the origin of 'Pulling a Rope' in Ludlow dates from the reign of Henry VI and the Wars of the Roses, when Ludlow's population, under siege, was divided: part in favour of the King and part for the Duke of York; which I suppose is as good a reason as any for tugging away at a rope.

Tournament.
(Harl. ms)

2. Racing and Endeavour

It has been suggested that horse racing, as opposed to chariot racing, was first introduced at Olympic Games about the middle of the 7th century BC and that forms of Chariot Racing were performed at an early time possibly from about 3000 BC when the War Chariot is thought to have been evolved. This might at first sight seem strange as it is obvious that the horse came before the chariot, but it must be remembered that stirrups were late in being invented and it was easier to drive a horse from a chariot than to ride at full gallop without stirrups.

Horse racing in Britain probably originated during the Roman occupation when Lucius Septimus Severus brought Arabian steeds to this country.

In the 12th century William Lion founded a race called the Lanark Silver Bell, an event still held. Silver bells were traditional prizes for horse races, being replaced by cups and plates only in the reign of Charles II. Another Silver Bell race was held at Chester in 1539 (said by some authorities to be 1540), in which the bell is recorded to be worth three shillings and six pence. This particular event was later to become known as the St. George's Race. The Chester Bell was 'dedicated to the Kinge, being double gilt with the King's arms upon it', and carried, 'upon a septer in pompe and before him a noise of trumpets in pompe'.

Apart from the Lanark Silver Bell, one of the oldest horse races held in Britain is the Kipling Cotes over a five mile course near Market Weighton, Yorkshire, a course which passes through several parishes. The race takes place on the 3rd Thursday in March each year, starting at noon. It is said that the first Kipling Cotes was run in 1519 but it was not until 1618 that Lord Burlington left a legacy from the interest of which the winners' prize money is paid.

Horse Racing has been said to be the 'Sport of Kings' and this is indeed true; Edwards II, III, and IV, as well as Henry VIII, all had running horses as distinct from war chargers; nothwithstanding, after the time of Richard I, horse racing as a sport declined almost into oblivion. It was James I who brought horse racing back into prominence by buying the Markham Arabian and building stables at Newmarket. This was the birth

Epsom

of the modern era of horse racing, although Newmarket can rightly claim to be the home of the sport as we know it.

The horses from which all British 'thoroughbred' bloodstock can be traced were the Darley Arabian (imported about 1704), the Godolphin Arabian (imported from Paris in 1729), and the Byerly Turk. It is thought by some authorities that these stallions were put to English mares, while other opinions suggest that Eastern mares were imported.

The foundation of the Jockey Club in the 1750s was a landmark in British racing. It was formed after a meeting of the patrons of sport at what was one of the greatest of all sport's gathering places: The Star and Garter, in Pall Mall, long since disappeared. It was here also that the Laws of Cricket were revised in 1774.

In 1774, at either The Salutation Inn or The Red Lion, Doncaster, a party met to arrange the staging of a race for three year olds. The company included Lt. 'Jack' Anthony St Leger who suggested that the race be run over a two mile course in his grounds. This was duly done on 4 September 1776 and, in the gentleman's honour, the race was called the St Leger Sweepstake. The winner of this first in the classic series was Lord Rockingham's Alabaculia.

34

Steeplechase

The Derby, a race for three-year-olds, was conceived at a party given by the Earl of Derby in 1779 at his home at Lambert's Oaks, Woodmansterne, Epsom, Surrey. Under similar circumstances a year earlier he had thought of The Oaks, the classic race for fillies, the name Oaks being inspired by Lord Derby's house.

The Derby was first run in 1780 (won by Sir Claude Bunbury on Diamed), and since 1784 it has been held at the Epsom Race Course which, in those days, was known as Banstead Down. Epsom was a popular spa resort with Londoners, and it was soon the fashion that every spa town should have its own race course.

There has been little change in jockey's clothing since the 17th century, and colours became compulsory as early as 1762. In the old days jockeys wore tight trousers, quilted silk jackets in bright colours and a cap. In the mid-18th century, according to the *Gentleman's Recreation* magazine, riders should be attired in

Jackets of coloured silk, or of white Holland, as being very advantageous to the spectator. Your waistcoat and drawers must be made close to your body, and on your head a cap tied. Let your boots be gartered up fast and your spurs must be of good metal.

35

Eclipse. The greatest race horse of all time. Born of Arab stock in 1764 and died in 1789. Although this magnificent horse won so many races, and the amount of money won in betting on it is inestimable, only about £2,000 was collected in actual prizemoney

In the days before female emancipation it is surprising that the ladies took such an active part in horse racing. The Ladies' Plate at Ripon of 1725 has been recorded and we have several other examples of the fair sex's prowess at riding. For example, in 1804 a race was undertaken, as a result of a wager for 500 guineas, over a four mile course at the York August meeting. Mrs Thornton, for that was the lady's name, was riding her husband's horse, Vingarillo, and her opponent, a Mr Flint, was riding his own horse, Thornville. I am sorry to have to relate that Mrs Thornton lost.

Marathon horse racing has always attracted sportsmen. In 1822 a race was held from Burford to Gloucester and back, a distance of 62 miles. The time taken by the two contestants was seven hours and, not surprisingly, both horses died shortly after the race. The wager that prompted the race was a mere 25 guineas!

Derby Winner,
c. 1830

In 1759 Mr J. Shafto undertook to ride 59 miles in two hours at the Newmarket Race Course. He completed the distance in 1hr 49mins and 15secs, and, it is said, to have won over £15,000 in so doing, but using up 10 horses in the process.

In 1752, some years before England's first recorded Steeplechase (in fact the same year of a mention of such an event in Ireland), Sir Charles Turner made a wager with the Earl of March for 1,000 guineas that he would successfully undertake what was called a Leaping Match on a fell near Richmond, Yorkshire. The conditions were that Sir Charles should ride 10 miles within one hour during which time he was to take 40 *leaps,* each leap to be over 1yd, 1qr and 7ins high fences. He is reported to have achieved this on a galloway in 36mins.

No summary of horse racing would be complete without mention of one of the greatest sportsmen of all time: George Osbaldeston. Of course it would be hard to think of any early

19th century sport at which the squire did not excel. In 1831 he undertook a match against time on the Round Course at Newmarket. He was 45 years old and recovering from a broken leg, but he completed 200 miles in 8hrs 42mins, using 27 horses and changing every 4 miles. After his achievement this stalwart celebrated by drinking through the night at The Rutland Arms.

Nobody really knows how and where steeplechasing began, but according to one story, it started in the early 18th century when a landowner, entertaining guests after a day in the hunting field, went to the door and shouted a challenge that he would race anyone to the church steeple for a cask of rum.

As its name implies, steeplechasing in its early form was a trial of speed across country between two or more horses with a church steeple as a goal. It is believed that some form of Steeple-chasing was run at Newmarket during the reign of James I but information is lacking. Miss Dorothy Laird, Features Editor of the *Racing Information Bureau,* tells me that most authorities consider that any racing which James I initiated at Newmarket whilst hunting there was on the flat.

It is probable that steeplechasing originated in Ireland and there are records of this form of racing in that country from 1752. In one of these races the first prize was a hogshead of claret, a pipe of port and a quarter cask of Jamaican rum.

The first known steeplechase in England was held in 1790 from Barkby Holt to Billesden Coplow and back, a distance of 8 miles. In that same year, and also in Leicestershire, there was a race from Melton Mowbray to Dalby Wood.

The Grand Liverpool Steeplechase was first held in 1837. This was the event which was later to become known as the Grand National.

Surprisingly, London had a steeplechase course in 1841. This was known as the Hippodrome and was situated on a site in existing Ladbroke Grove.

Trotting Horse

Although in its present form Trotting is a comparatively new sport — the first recorded race in America being held in 1818 — one can see a relationship between a horse trotting and pulling a 40lb *sulky,* and a horse of Rome at full gallop around the arena with a racing chariot in tow. Trotting may indeed be an ancient form of horse racing, for in the 1930s some baked clay bricks were excavated in Asia Minor which gave very precise instructions on how to train horses to trot while pulling a cart or a chariot. These bricks have been dated at about 1350 BC.

There is some evidence of chariots being used for racing in India at the time of the Aryan phase, indeed, before such style of racing is thought to have taken place in ancient Greece and

Rome. In Rome, genuine and serious chariot races were held in the Circus Maximus and only the novelty races were held in the Colosseum — races that involved chariots drawn by ostriches, camels, oryxes and other unusual creatures.

Roman charioteers were mainly slaves, although there were more than a few freemen who drove in hope of riches; Juvenal wrote of one such charioteer, called Diocles, as having an income one hundred times more than that of a senator.

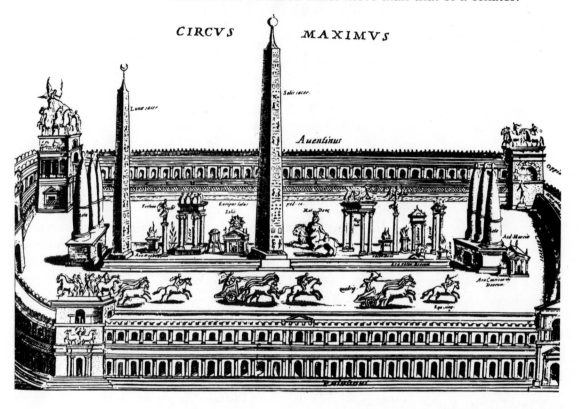

Roman Chariot Race

The racing in the various parts of the Roman Empire was managed and organised by several very large co-operatives, with fleets of ships, and often building and owning even the barrack blocks in the outpost settlements, the money being forthcoming from thousands of investors. Hippomania — horse madness — was the name given to the hysterical excitement shown by the crowd at chariot races. After one particular race the crowd, who did not accept the judge's decision, burned down the Circus Maximus. It was this act which caused the law which stipulated that all amphitheatres had to be built from stone.

Early chariot races are believed to have been run with the drivers aiming and racing to a mark some distance away,

Roman Horse and
Chariot in bronze.
1st century AD.

around which they circled and returned to the starting point.

This method of heading for a mark and returning to the starting place was used by the Kirghiz cattle breeders of the Kerchese Steppes, in a kind of horse race that was run to decide on who would take a girl who had reached marriageable age. The girl was given a distance start and all the suitors gave chase. The contestant who pulled the girl from her horse before the finish, or the one who was judged by the elders to have put up the bravest performance, won the girl. After the race the girl was allowed to retaliate by galloping after the men and lashing out with her whip.

Robust traditional horse races still continue in various parts of the world. One particularly rough bareback race over cobblestones, is held twice yearly, in July and August, at the Italian town of Sienna. The race is called the Palio and is run around the town square. The name *palio* is from the Latin for the silk banner which is presented to the district of the town — the *contrade* — from which the winner has been entered. It is said to have begun in 1482 as a custom to celebrate the return of *reformer citizens* to the government. In the old days the Palio was only one event in the celebrations which included Tournaments, Bull Baiting and Buffalo Fights, but now only the horse race remains.

Serious athletic contests have had a somewhat chequered history, declining in popularity in favour of humorous competitions and emerging again to capture an enthusiastic following.

It has been said, and probably rightly, that athletic contests date from the Greek Olympic Games, and these are very ancient, being reorganised in the 9th century BC by Iphitus of Elis. Although there are traces of Greek Games being performed as early as c.1370 BC, the first Olympic Games for which there are any records were held in 776 BC, when Coroebus won the Stadion (foot race). Other events at these early Olympic Games included Long Jump; the Throwing of

40

Voelker's Gymnastics

the Discus or Quoit; Wrestling in the gymnasia arena, called the Palaestra; Diaulos, running twice the length of the Stadium; Pentathlon, running, leaping, throwing the quoit and javelin; Pancratium, meaning the *complete contest*, the contestants being allowed to use any means to overcome their adversary, including strangulation; Chariot Races, foot races in heavy armour; contests for herald and trumpeters; and gymnastics.

The traditional prizes at the early Olympic Games were wreaths of sacred olives which were said to have been planted by Hercules.

The games died in the 4th century AD by order of the Emperor Theodosius — a year fixed by some historians as 393 and by others as a year later. It was not until 1896 that they were revived in Athens, the long-distance race being held between the ancient battlefield of Marathon and the Averoff Stadium.

Running Footmen, servants who used to run alongside the carriages of the nobility, often took part in competitions motivated by large wagers of their masters. Samuel Pepys describes two such races: one took place in 1660 in Hyde Park and another in 1663 on Banstead Downs, between Lee, the Duke of Richmond's footman, and a man named Tyler, a famous runner of the day. Lee won the race despite the bets of the King and the Duke of York on Tyler.

41

The Duke of Queensberry ('Old Q'), who died in 1810, was one of the last to keep Running Footmen. One of his runners was pitched in a race to Windsor against the Duke of Marlborough driving a phaeton. The footman barely lost and died shortly afterwards.

The Running Footman was at one time a widespread inn sign, and in a number of instances has evolved into the Running Man.

One of the first 19th century Athletics Meetings in England was organised by a Major Mason in 1807 in association with the Necton Guild in Norfolk. The events at this meeting included wrestling, jumping in sacks, and foot races.

This does not mean, of course, that between the end of the ancient Olympics and the revival of athletics in the 19th century, competitions of a physical nature were completely unknown: The Tailtin Games held in Ireland are claimed to date back two or three thousand years and they have certainly been held for some centuries. Similarly the Highland Games at Braemar, Aboyne, and at other places in Scotland have a long history. These brave and colourful sights do not only feature feats of athletic prowess, but bagpipe playing, reel dancing, and sword dancing. The sports are traditionally Scottish and, apart from running, long and high jumps, and hop, step and jump (the triple jump), there are Putting the Stone, Throwing the 56lb weight, and Throwing the Hammer. The latter is thought to be of considerable age and was certainly known in the time of Henry VII; for centuries it has been a favourite sport in Scotland and Ireland. Finally there is that enormous feat of strength, Tossing the Caber, a tapering pine tree between 16 and 20ft tall with its branches lopped.

A form of Cross-Country Running that was popular until recent years was that of Hare and Hounds, or Paper Chase. This involved one, two, and sometimes more runners starting ahead of the rest of the field and scattering a trail of torn paper. The others then set off at intervals and attempted to overtake the *hares*. This form of pursuit sport died in this country with the introduction of legislation prohibiting the deposit of litter. Charles Dickens mentioned paper chases in *Household Words* (1856). Two years earlier, junior army officers engaged in Paper Chases as a recreation in the Crimean War.

I am indebted to Mr M.L. Charlesworth, a Senior Master, for his description of the unique Royal Shrewsbury School Hunt. It is a most interesting organisation and goes on today in much the same way as it did for most of the 19th century, viz., the school captain is called the *Huntsman* and dresses for the runs

Hurdling at the Oxford v Cambridge Sports

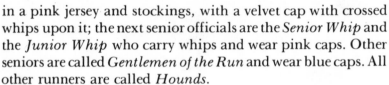

Mountaineering and Equipment

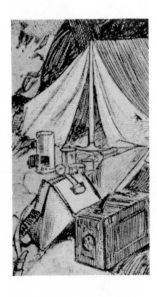

in a pink jersey and stockings, with a velvet cap with crossed whips upon it; the next senior officials are the *Senior Whip* and the *Junior Whip* who carry whips and wear pink caps. Other seniors are called *Gentlemen of the Run* and wear blue caps. All other runners are called *Hounds*.

The terminology of foxhunting is used throughout.

Cross-Country Runs are taken every week in winter and although the courses have changed somewhat with the encroachment of suburbia, old names of runs are preserved. This running club was certainly in existence in the decade 1820-30; and the *Hound Books* which record the runs constitute an unbroken account from 1842 to the present day. It is believed there is no other cross-country running club with such a continuous record.

Gymnastics in an organised form are said to have originated with the Greeks, coupled with moral and general education. When boys showed prowess, their training in general education was undertaken by the State. Plato considered physical education to be of great importance, as did Prodicus and Hippocrates in 400 BC. *Gymnastics* and *athletics* were synonymous and both activities included running, leaping and throwing. The Romans, at the height of their power, were keen gymnasts, the exercise forming part of the social activities at the baths.

The real revival of gymnastics was in Germany in 1811 when F. Ludwig Jahn established his Turnplatze in Berlin. Two years later, Ling in Sweden founded his gymnasium and developed a branch known as Swedish Drill. In 1825 Voelker, a student of Jahn, opened a gymnasium at 1 Union Place, New Road, near St James Park, and another at Fontain's Riding School, Worship Street, Finsbury Square. Voelker had come to England after having a gymnasium in Berlin which he had had to abandon because of the war in Germany. His fees in London were high for the period: £1 per month, £2.10s for three months, £4 for six months, and £6 for one year. His courses of instruction included running, leaping with or without a pole, climbing masts, ropes and ladders, exercise on parallel bars, vaulting and fencing.

Why anyone should want to climb mountains is a mystery to some people. One of the best explanations I know is in a book called *At Grips With Everest,* in which Stanley Snaith writes:

Mountain climbing is a sport. It is not practised for rewards, for fame, or even primarily for scientific purposes. Like any other sport, it has its own reward. A swimmer does not plunge into the sea at Dover because he thinks that is the easiest or safest way of reaching France. The fox-hunter is not chasing his dinner. Sport is independent of practical results. It is a personal thing. To the mountaineer it is not merely the attainment of the summit that counts, but the exercise of craft, knowledge, nerve and sinew in achieving that goal.

The first recorded ascent of a high mountain was that of the 7,000ft Mont Aigville near Grenoble in 1492 — the year of Columbus' voyage to the New World — by order of Charles VIII of France, but this was an action at the whim of the monarch and cannot be said to have anything to do with sport. It was organised like a battle and the dozen or so climbers stayed on the mountain for a week, baptising the summit during that time.

The first climb of a snow mountain was that of the Titlis in 1739 by a monk, whose name has unfortunately not survived the passage of time. Sir Alfred Lunn in *A Century of Mountaineering,* does not mention this climb but does refer to an ascent of the Titlis by two peasants in 1744.

Water sports and activities were not popular until the craze for sea-water bathing started in the Regency period. In fact swimming was positively discouraged during Elizabeth I's reign to the extent that at Cambridge University under-graduates were forbidden to swim and threatened with penalties of flogging or expulsion should they do so.

Competitive swimming began around 1837 in London when
there were some half a dozen fresh water pools built for the
purpose. It was in that same year that the Boston (Lincolnshire)
Sea Water Company advertised their third season of bathing
with facilities including cold, warm, and vapour baths. Even
so, it was not until 1869 that the Amateur Swimming
Association was formed. Even in this country — a nation of
seamen — water sports in both sea and fresh water were
considered as rather an uncomfortable way of enjoying oneself,
and swimming was to be engaged in only as a means of survival
after falling overboard.

Since Captain Matthew Webb first swam the English
Channel on 24-25 August 1875, it has become an annual

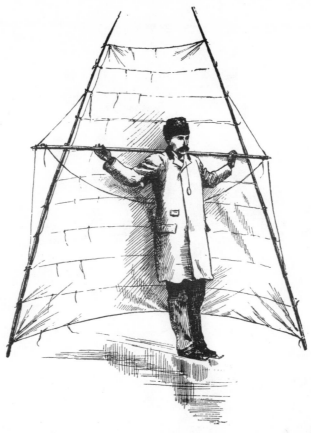

Sailing on skates

The *Icicle*

sporting programme in the latter part of the summer, with dozens of swimmers gathering on both sides of the Channel.

Previously, in June 1874, Webb swam from Dover to the N.E. Varne, a distance of 9 nautical miles (11 statute); a year later he swam from Blackwall Pier to Gravesend Town Pier, 16 nautical miles.

Bicycle Racing in its road form can be traced back, as far as Britain is concerned, to 1869 when Messrs. Mayall, Turner and Spencer attempted to ride from Clapham to Brighton. Mayall arrived alone after about 16 hours. Also in that year, it is believed, occurred the first Track (originally known as *Path*) Race for Velocipedes in Britain; this was on a track built for the event at the Crystal Palace. In France, the start was a year earlier on 31 May 1868, on a 2 kilometre course at the Parc de St Cloud, Paris.

It is probable that the idea of sailing craft fitted with skates originated in the Netherlands during the 18th century as a means of transport for goods in winter months. In the following hundred years the sport of racing these yachts on ice gained popularity — mainly, of course, where there were large tracts of ice available, such as the Gulf of Finland and the

Skating at St Ives,
Huntingdon

Hendelopen
'Priksleedje'

Sleigh-sailing

A Friesland skate

English skates

Hudson River. The first ice yachting club formed in the U.S.A. was inaugurated in 1861.

Thought to be considerably older than the ice yacht and probably its immediate ancestor, is the Sand Yacht or Land Yacht. It is again credited to those great users of wind power, the Dutch, and the land yacht has been mentioned as a means of transport as far back as the 16th century-

The earliest skis that have so far been found were unearthed in the Fenno-Scandian bog and are believed to have been made about 2500 BC. As early as 1767 the Norwegians held military skiing competitions in Oslo but it was not until 1843 that true sporting events were held in Tromsø . In those days the ski was known as the Norwegian snowshoe.

Contrary to popular belief, the ski was late in arriving in the Alps and it is not until the 1880s that the idea was imported. Before that, in the 1850s the ski was popular in California, and in Australia in the 1870s when the Kiandra Snowshoes Club was founded.

The greatest sporting ski event currently to take place is the Swedish Vasaloppet race in which there are sometimes more than 6,000 contestants racing over a 54 mile cross-country course. At the beginning of the 16th century, when Sweden was occupied by the Danes, a man named Gustav Eriksson attempted to raise a fight for freedom. Unsuccessful in his early attempts, he was forced to make a dash for Norway and

49

Speed skating race,
Amsterdam, 1889

American Toboggan

Bob-Sled

Canadian Toboggan

sanctuary. He was captured by his pursuers at Salen in the province of Dalecarlia. His later campaigns were more successful; the Danes were defeated and the rebel Eriksson became King Gustav Vasa I. The Vasaloppet commemorates this hero.

The home of Toboggan and Bobsleigh sports is rightly considered to be Switzerland. It was at Davos am Platz in the Swiss canton of Grisors that English visitors saw Swiss children riding down slopes on sleds carrying their family coat of arms. It was thought that here was the basis of a new sport and the Davos Run was conceived, using a path from the Belvedere Hotel to the nearby road. Part way down the run was an aspen tree, the site of many a spill. Toboggans in those early days were steered by short sticks about 8ins long in the manner of skiing.

St Moritz became a great winter sports resort in the 1880s. This was the home of the annual International Toboggan Race which was first held in the winter of 1882-83 on the newly constructed Cresta Run. This was on 12 February 1883, with 21 competitors from England, Germany, Holland, Switzerland and countries of the British Empire.

Toboggans engaged in these early events were of the Swiss Coaster (or Schlitti) type. The bobsleigh with its steerable runners was the invention of S. Whitney in 1889.

The Cresta Run

The Schlitti or Swiss
Coaster

The name 'toboggan' is derived from the American Indian word *odabaggan*, meaning to sledge, and there is a tradition that the Coughnawaga Indians around the Ontario district used toboggans as a form of amusement. Tobogganing grew in popularity as a sport in Canada and the U.S.A. after the 1880s, and in some parts of the States there were even built imitation runs using grassy slopes. In the USSR it is traditional for the track to be over ground on which there are rises as well as falls. Racing is usually between pairs, as opposed to the Bobsleigh events in which the runs are timed.

In 1869, on the site of a building being demolished near London Wall, pieces of bone were found which were considered to date from the Roman occupation and which could well have been used as primitive ice skates. The early

51

historian, William FitzStephen relates in his *Description of London,* published in 1180:

When the great fenne or moore (which watereth the walles of the citie on the north side) is frozen, many young men play upon the yce. Some stryding as wide as they may, doe slide swiftly. Some tye bones to their feete, and under their heeles, and shoving themselves by a little picked staffe doe slide as swiftly as a birde flyeth in the aire, or an arrow out of a crossbow.

It seems fairly clear that originally skates were made from wood or bone and the skaters propelled themselves along by means of a single stick with an iron point.

It is thought that the earliest metal skates, probably the invention of the Dutch, were not used until early in the 17th century.

Edinburgh claims the distinction of having the world's first skating club which was formed in 1742. The London Skating Club was founded in 1830 and this body laid down a set of rules concerning the figures to be skated. In those days up to ten skaters took part in the set figures. As early as 1842 an artificial ice rink was opened at the Baker Street Bazaar, called the Alpine Lake. The substance of the *lake* was crystallised alum mixed with grease and hog's lard, salts of soda and melted sulphur; somewhat disagreeable to the skaters as falls had the most unpleasant consequences.

Later, in 1865, an artificial ice made by a process using carbonic acid and brine was patented, but it was not until 1870 that William E. Newton adapted the invention of Matthew Julius Bujac for an ice rink using the refrigeration process of circulation of ammoniacal gas, ether, or carbonic acid.

In 1870 too, Professor John Gangee invented another process for making ice by the abstraction of latent heat, and by 1876 refrigeration techniques had reached a stage that made indoor skating on real ice commercially feasible, and in that year several rinks were opened. It was Gangee's process that was used on the Rusholme Ice Rink at Manchester which was opened in 1876. There was a rink at the Floating Baths, Charing Cross; the Empress Rink at Tichbourne Street, Piccadilly Circus, where the Great National Skating Contest was held; and another in Chelsea. Numbers did not grow, however, and in 1897 London still had only three rinks: The Niagara Hall, The National Skating Palace, and the Prince's Skating Club, the aforementioned three already having gone out of action.

Roller Skating was regarded as a substitute for Ice Skating when climatic conditions did not permit the real thing. The first roller skate is reputed to have been invented about 1760 by Joseph Merlin, a Belgian from Huy near Liege, but it did not prove to be very satisfactory. Merlin came to England with the Spanish Ambassador and here demonstrated his invention. To quote from *Belgravia:*

Supplied with a pair of these and a violin, he mixed in the motley group of the celebrated Mrs Cornelly's masquerade at Carlisle House, Soho Square when, not having provided the means of retarding his velocity or commanding its duration, he impelled himself against a mirror of more than £500 value, dashed it to atoms, broke his instrument to pieces, and wounded himself severely.

In 1823, R.J. Tyers, a Piccadilly fruiterer, invented and patented a roller skate. It consisted of five rollers in line, the middle one being the largest and the others progressively smaller. It was not until 1865 or 1866 that James Plimpton of New York patented a reliable skate, whereupon the sport began to gain popularity.

Without doubt, the oldest rowing event in existence in Britain is the Doggatt Coat and Badge. Irish actor, Thomas Doggatt (William Hone spells the name *Doggat*), sponsored this contest in 1715 to commemorate the accession of George I.

Doggatt died in 1721 and left a legacy to provide a prize anually. This consisted of a scarlet (some early accounts refer to it as orange) livery coat with silver buttons; on the left arm is a silver badge with the prancing horse of Hanover and the word *Liberty.* The race is run as near as possible to 1 August (the date of George I's accession in 1714) from The Old Swan Pier, London Bridge, to Cadogan Pier, Chelsea, always against the tide.

It is now under the administration of the Worshipful Company of Fishmongers, in whose charge Doggatt's legacy is held. The contestants are six Thames watermen who have completed their apprenticeship during the past twelve months.

The Coat and Badge was won by Jack Broughton in 1730, the prize fighter who compiled the first set of rules to standardise the sport.

Rowing was late in becoming an accepted sport and until the 19th century it was considered an activity suitable only for youths and river watermen — a hangover from the time of galley slaves, no doubt. By 1800 it had become more accepted as a gentleman's pastime and in 1825 the Oxford and Cambridge Universities started their Bumping Races, using boats with

Doggatt's Coat and Badge. The prize rowed for by Thames watermen since 1715

53

Rowing on the Thames. (Woodcut by Henry Dutt Linton, 1815-1899)

four and six oars. This is a form of race in which the boats start at 160ft intervals; a specification decided upon because of the limited width of the river, which prevented satisfactory racing of boats in side-by-side positions, although this had been attempted in the early days. Once a boat is bumped from the rear the crew have to withdraw from the race.

1829 was a landmark in the history of rowing for sport. It was in that year that Oxford challenged Cambridge to an 8-oar race on the river Thames. Oxford won. Also in that year was rowed the first in a series of annual races between Eton and Winchester schools, held from Putney to Hammersmith and back. However, the series was short lived and was abandoned in 1864.

Seven years were to elapse before the next University race, and it did not become an annual event until 1856. The Henley shopkeepers and traders were so pleased with the additional trade brought by spectators to the early races that they decided to hold an annual Regatta, separate from any future University event, and so the Henley Regatta was born in 1839. But this was not the first of Regattas. There had been sea-water Regattas since the Regency period when the seaside became fashionable. The first Regatta to be held on the Thames was probably in 1775 near the Ranelagh Gardens (established in 1742 near

54

where the Battersea Pleasure Gardens are now to be found) but this was a rather primitive affair as boating had not become an accepted sport.

As mentioned before, the Oxford and Cambridge race became an annual event in 1856, but the now familiar Putney to Mortlake course was not fixed until 1862.

Canoeing is distinguished from rowing and sculling in that a canoe paddle spoons away at the water instead of passing through a rollock which acts as a fulcrum. It began as a sport in 1865 when John MacGregor took his oak and cedar canoe, *Rob Roy*, on a 1,000 mile journey along continental waterways.

Yachting is said to date from 1720, when the Water Club of the Harbour of Cork was formed, but not much progress was made until 1812 when the Royal Yacht Squadron was founded with fifty members. On the other hand, we must not forget that in 1662, Charles II raced his brother, the Duke of York, on the Thames for a £100 wager.

It was Queen Victoria's patronage of the Royal Yacht Squadron that stamped yachting as the fashionable sport it has since become, with Cowes, Isle of Wight, the accepted home. All around the coast of Britain in Victorian times yachting was becoming a popular and fashionable pastime. One centre on the east coast was Boston, Lincolnshire, where in 1858 the Boston Yacht Club had 13 yachts and about 100 members.

By 1846 yachting was established in the United States, and in 1851 the U.S. Schooner *America* crossed the Atlantic to compete against British craft. It was victorious and the award, originally called the *Queen's Cup*, went over the ocean to remain there to this day.

The America Cup

Oxford and Cambridge Boat Race

55

Cricket Match at Wittersham, Kent

3. Ball Games

Ever since it was discovered that a spherical object could be rolled, thrown, caught, kicked and hit with a club, ball games have been in fashion. In this chapter we consider most of the games that can be played with a ball in motion, either by striking, catching or throwing.

The first reference we find to Cricket is that of John Derrick who, in 1598, is reported as saying, 'at Guildeforde he did runne and play there at Crickett'. Earlier we have mention of John Leek, Chaplain of Prince Edward, the king's son, playing a game called Creag in the year 1300. Although it is impossible now to discover the nature of this game, it may have been a forerunner of Cricket.

The earliest form of cricket of which we have definite knowledge was played with a single set of stumps, rather like the game played by children at the seaside. This single wicket cricket remained in popularity for many years as a gambling game, usually with less than five players taking part on each side. The number of players was not fixed, and depended on how many people wanted to play. The ball was rolled, not 'hurled' over-arm as it is today, and that is why, of course, the action is called *bowling*. It was not until 1864 that over-arm delivery was officially allowed — a style which was adopted by women, who found it more convenient than under-arm because of the voluminous skirts of the period. Women, in fact, have been attracted to cricket for longer than is popularly believed. There is a record of a ladies' match being played at Gosden Common, Guildford, in 1745, between 'eleven maids of Hambledon and eleven maids of Bramley'.

The stumps at the beginning of the 18th century were two sticks driven into the ground, 2ft apart and about 1ft high. On top of these stumps was placed a thin twig. Each player in turn, except the captain, bowled to the batsman. With five players a side this meant four balls to the over. The bats used in those days were implements which looked like hockey sticks with thick ends. So many disputes arose from claims and denials that the ball had passed between the stumps that, shortly after the laws had been defined, a third, and middle stump was added.

The laws under which cricket was played, in common with all other games, varied from area to area, and it was as late as

England v Australia,
Lords 1884

W.G. Grace

1774 that standardised laws were drawn up. By this time the game had evolved into the 'double' form, with stumps at each end of the pitch — although it was specified that the number of stumps had to be two. The number of players in a team was fixed at eleven by the time of the introduction of the 1774 laws. One interesting law of 1774 was that related to the choice of pitch: the captain of the side that lost the toss of a coin selected a spot on the field as a wicket; the captain of the other side would then select the position of the other wicket to be placed within a circle of 30yds radius.

At the beginning of the 19th century cricket was the only team game in England with standardised rules. It was also early in the list of professional games and it was in 1806 that the first Gentlemen versus Players match was played.

The golden days of Stool-Ball were between the 15th and 18th centuries. This game, which superficially looks like a form of cricket, probably has a different but equally antique origin. In the Middle Ages it was popular with women and may have been originated by milkmaids when relaxing after milking; a three-legged milking stool was placed in the middle of a field and stones were thrown at it. One player at a time defended the stool with her hands and person, scores being made by either the attackers making a hit, or the defender catching or deflecting the stone. It was, to say the least, a rough game for women, and

Cricket in the late
18th century

over the years it took on a more gentle nature with a ball being
used in place of a stone, and a club employed instead of the poor
unfortunate having to defend the stool with her body. Of
course, the rules of stool-ball varied from area to area. In some
places the stool was defended with a stick or battledore-shaped
bat, while in other places they persisted in using the hands and
body to knock away the ball. In most places, every time the ball
was hit away it counted one point for the batsman and, of
course, if the stool was hit, he or she was out.

Trap Ball or Bat and Trap is said to have been played in Kent,
particularly East Kent, since the 14th century, and played by

A Ladies' Cricket
Match

SCHOOL CRICKET VARIATIONS

School	Name of Game	Style
Christ's Hospital	Feeder Cricket	Combination of Baseball and Cricket
Leas School, Hoylake	Spoofles	Teams of 5 players, 4-ball overs. Single wicket.
Loretto School	Puddex, Puddocks or Podex	Played with a tennis ball. Thick round bats. Pitch 14yds long. Each batsman retires on making 25 runs.
Marlborough College	Snobs	String covered ball. Solid wooden wicket.

Spoofles Cricket Field

The ball is bowled from single stump A. To score the batsman has to run to single stump B and return to his crease

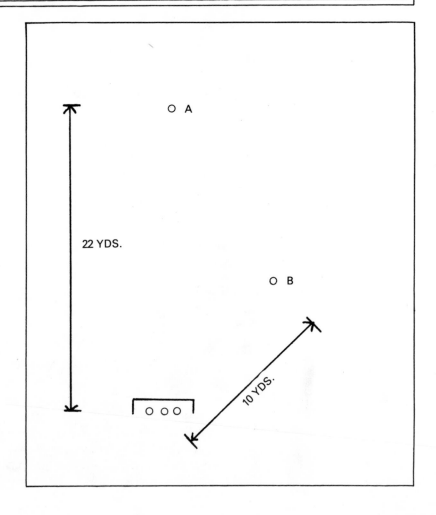

22 YDS.

○ A

○ B

10 YDS.

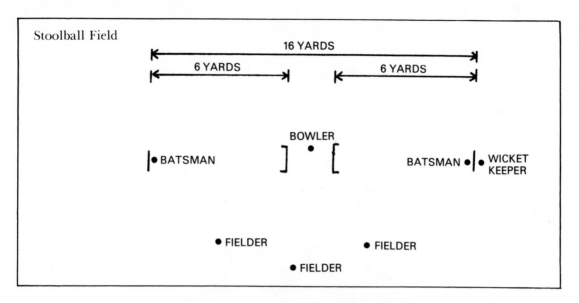

Stoolball Field

pilgrims on their way to Becket's tomb at Canterbury. It is still played at a number of public houses in and around the town.

The accepted Bat and Trap pitch is 21yds long and 13ft 6ins wide. The teams are of ten players aside. The 'bowling' end is bordered by two posts 12ft apart, behind which there is a semi-circular fielding margin. At the batting end there is a small see-saw called a 'shoe'. This see-saw is about 3ft long, with a spoon-shaped recess at one end in which the ball is placed. The other end of this see-saw is struck by the batsman with a short club, whereupon the ball flies into the air and is hit with the club. In front of the shoe stands the 'trap', a hinged tile. To make a score the ball has to pass between the two posts at the 'bowling' end. The 'fielders' stand in front of these posts and attempt to catch balls struck by batsmen of the opposing team. Another way of being out is for a fielder to bowl the ball at the trap which may not be defended. When the trap is hit the batsman is out. There are, of course, many local variations in rules for Bat and Trap, one of which is the method of scoring by which the batsman has to guess the distance the ball is hit, gaining points for a correct guess and losing points for a mistake.

Similar to Bat and Trap was a game by the name of Strike Up and Lay Down. In this game, any number of players took part, each batting in turn while all the others tried to force him out. The batsman had a ball and a stick about 18ins long, and stood in the middle of a small circle marked on the ground. He threw up the ball and hit it as far as he could. There were several ways of being declared out: the batsman could be caught or, if the ball was picked up by a fielder, the batsman had to place his bat

on the ground inside the circle, and the player who picked up the ball had to try to hit the bat from where he was standing. A batsman could also be out if he failed to hit the ball three times in succession.

Knurr (Knur or Nurr) and Spell, is the North of England version of the Bat and Trap game, and in the late 19th century it was considered to be a kind of poor man's golf but it faded in popularity about the turn of the century. The equipment consisted of a throwing device called a 'spell' of which various kinds have been devised, from a sling-gibbet type — called the 'gallus' — to several see-saw types.

The missile, called the 'knurr' or, more rarely, the 'guinea' was shaped something like a lemon with a short snout and tail, and about the size of a golfball. The material was a hardwood

Below: Club Ball. 14th and 15th centuries

62

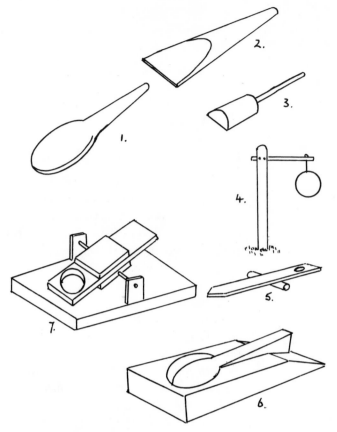

Knurr and Spell Equipment.
  1 and 2.   Types of Bat, Pommel, Tripstick or Pumstick.
       3.   A Pommel c. 1870. Exhibited at the Castle Museum, York.
       4.   Gallows or sling-type Spell.
       5.   Tipping Spell c. 1800.
  6 and 7.   19th century Spells.

such as holly. In some versions of the game, which were
introduced from about 1870, the knurr took the form of a glazed
pottery ball made from special clay and fired at a high
temperature. These measured $\frac{7}{8}$in. in diameter and weighed
$\frac{1}{2}$oz. Seventy years earlier, Joseph Strutt described the 18th
century knurr as being made from leather. Apart from these
materials, it is believed that staghorn was used in some areas.
The bat was called the 'pommel', 'tripstick' or 'pum stick',
depending on the area, and consisted of a springy handle of
hickory with a head of compressed beech.

In play the knurr was placed in a circular opening at the
lower end of the tilting part of the spell. The upper end of the
tilting part was struck by the bat, which caused the knurr to
shoot upwards. The batsman then struck the knurr as far as he

63

Bandy-Ball, 14th
century

could, when the members of the opposing team attempted to
catch it. In one version of the game the batsman made runs by
chasing to a peg, while in others a 100yds knock counted as five
points. Sometimes the distances for each hit were added
together and the total credited to the batsman's team, while in
yet other versions the knurr had to be knocked into holes in the
least number of strokes as in golf, or had to be hit into a marked
area nearby.

This group of games, Knurr and Spell in the northern
counties, and known as Bad i' th' Wood or Bungs and Barrels in
the Midlands, together with Tipcat, is said by some authorities
to be of Scandinavian origin. A kind of Bat and Trap, played on
ice and called Knattlier, is played in Scandinavian countries
and thought to be ancient. Be that as it may, the name of Knurr
and Spell is undoubtedly from the Dutch, *knorrenspel*,
knorren meaning to hum or buzz — the sound made by the
missile flying through the air — and *spel* meaning a game.

Tipcat, Cat, Nipcat, or Batonnet is a near relative to Knurr
and Spell, and Bat and Trap, but instead of a ball or lemon-
shaped knurr, the missile is a stick pointed at each end. The
'cat' stands pivoted on a brick or a stone. There are two basic
styles of the game, one known as Scores and the other as Long
Knock, but each depends on the length of the hit. Scores
involved throwing the cat to the batsman who had to hit it with
the other players running from mark to mark until it was

Ball Play, 14th
century

returned. Long Knock, as its name suggests, was a game in
which the batsman stood in the middle of a large circle and was
declared 'out' if he could not hit the cat outside the circle.

The word 'cat' constantly occurs in games of this type.
Another example is Cat and Dog, which is believed to be of
considerable antiquity. It involved three players, two of whom
defended holes in the ground about 13yds apart. Their task was
to hit away a piece of wood which the third player aimed at the
holes. The bats used were called 'dogs' and the missile was
known as the 'cat'.

The origin of the American game of Baseball is more obscure
than would appear at first sight. In the modern form it was the
invention of an army officer by the name of Abner Doubleday at
Cooperstown, New York in 1839, but its earlier roots are less
certain. It may have been derived from another American game,
One (or Two, or Three, or Four) Old Cat which, almost
without doubt, was a variation of the English or Scandinavian
Tipcat games. The resemblance of Baseball to the English
game of Rounders may or may not be coincidental, but it
certainly bears more than a superficial likeness. There is a
strange reference, without any method of play being
mentioned, to a game called Baseball in a children's book,
called *The Little Pretty Pocket Book*, published in England in
1744. To confuse the problem still more there was recently a
Russian newspaper article claiming that American Baseball

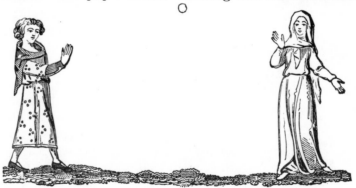

65

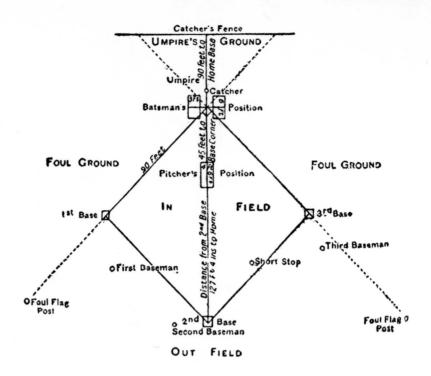

Baseball Field

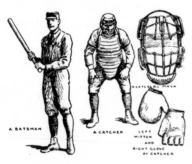

Baseball

had its origins in an old Russian game called *Beizbol*. All this being as it may, a game called Base-Ball or Baste-Ball was banned in the State of New Jersey in 1786 — forty three years before Doubleday invented his game of Baseball. In those days it was fashionable to ban sports and games that inflamed the emotions of the spectators, unless of course, the games happened to be favourites of the ruling class.

In 1845 Alexander J. Cartright laid down a set of rules for his team, the Knickerbocker Club of Hoboken. These were the foundations of the rules under which the modern American game is played.

Rounders was a widely popular game in England during the 18th century. Originally it was a free and easy game with no fixed number of players. It was played on a field marked out in a pentagon with five bases 15-20yds apart. Rules to regulate the game were drawn up when the Rounders Association of Liverpool and Vicinity, and the Scottish Rounders Association was formed in 1889.

No sport has served man so well as Football. When a diversion was needed to brighten the dull working week in the times of the industrial revolution, Football was there waiting to be developed into an organised sport. Factory, mill and pit owners were happy because to some extent it relieved the discontent that must have been felt by workers brought from

66

Street Football at Barnet, c.1775

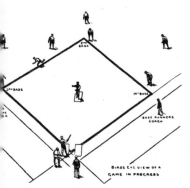

Baseball

the country to crowded town conditions in the little back-to-back houses. The men had an interest — a spectacle to watch and discuss for the rest of the week in taverns and at work.

Football had not always been such a good servant. For a long time it had been subject to legislation banning a brutal and destructive activity. In 1314 Edward II issued a proclamation forbidding the population 'to hustle over large balls' in the streets of the City of London, on account of the evils that might arise. A Statute of Edward III in 1349 ordered sheriffs to suppress football and, up to the time of Charles II, the game was considered unlawful. This was in the days when entire villages used to pit their male strength against each other in no-holds-barred combat. But in Galway, Ireland, it seems that the authorities looked on the game from a more kindly angle: in 1527, together with Archery, it was the only game exempt from prohibition.

For a long period of history there seems to have been an attraction to the mass game of kicking and carrying a ball, or some other object, over the ground. We know of a couple of football-type games in Roman times: Harpastum was a team ball game played on a rectangular field or pitch divided across the middle. That is about all we know factually about Harpastum; it is thought by some authorities that the object of the game was to seize the ball and carry it by some means or

Early Rugby
Football

other over a line on the ground at the rear of their opponents. Such a game may well have been introduced into Britain at the start of the Christian era.

The other Roman game was Paganica which appears to have been a considerable rough and tumble. The ball was placed in the centre of the pitch at each end of which was a baseline. Behind these lines the teams stood shoulder to shoulder. At a given signal an almighty rush was made for the ball. Peter Moss in *Sports and Pastimes Through the Ages* suggests these two Roman games were played by professionals. When it is considered that Gladiators and Charioteers were indeed professionals, it does seem reasonable to suppose that much of Rome's sport had this element.

In Britain the ball games continued on the rough and tough way through the centuries. The term *Camp-Ball,* it is believed, covered a number of varieties of a football game, one of which involved any number of people and had few, if any, rules. In this form of the game the ball was an animal bladder filled with dried peas. Injuries and deaths were common and the game was frowned upon by the ruling classes. Camp-Ball, or just simply *Camp,* as it was sometimes known, was played in East Anglia up to the 17th century or perhaps even later. It is believed that in this version there were two goals for each team, two at each end

SCHOOL FOOTBALL VARIATIONS

School	Name of Game	Style
Christ's Hospital	Housey Rugger Ends	Similar to Rugby rules but without scrummages. Teams take turns in kicking ball forwards, forcing opponents back until a goal can be dropped.
Edinburgh Academy	Hails, Played since 1824.	Rules amended in 1891. A form of Shinty but with some rugby rules.
Eton College	Wall Game.	Played only on 30 November. Teams: Collegers and Oppidans. 'Bosses' are scored by getting the ball to the opponent's 'calx' — marks on a door and a tree.
	Field Game.	Played since 1847. Throughout the Michaelmas Half Year. Combinations of 'handling' and 'dribbling' rules. Scores made by goals and 'rouges' — similar to rugby tries. Scrummage called a 'ram'.
Gordonstoun	Round Square Game	Played between 1936 and c 1960. A 'dribbling' game but using a rugby ball. Circular field. Two referees.
Harrow	Harrow Football	Played in Easter Term. Mainly 'dribbling' rules but, if caught and a call 'yards' is made, a free kick is awarded. Goals called 'bases'.
Radley College	Not Known	Played between c 1852 and 1882. Similar to Harrow Football.
Rugby	Rugby Football	Prior to 1823, very many players took part in the game. Kicks were made only forward and hand passes to the rear.
Shrewsbury	Douling.	Played up to c 1880. Rules not unlike rugby. Line out called a 'squash'. Game superceded by Association Football.
Westminster	Not Known	Rules not known but it seems that no teams were picked — the game being an individual effort.
Winchester College	Winchester Football	Played in Easter Term — Association Football at other times. 10ft high nets, called 'canvases', run along the sides of the 80 x 25yd field. Also ropes set alongside the 'canvases'. Ends of field marked with furrows, called 'worms'. Rules are complex.

of the field which was about 200yds long. There was an additional method of scoring: if the ball could not be passed to another member of the same team there was lost what was known as a *snotch,* with seven or nine *snotches* making up a game. The normal version of the game was called Savage Camp but there was another style known as Kicking Camp — whether this refers to kicking the ball or the other players is not clear!

It is technically wrong to describe these early games as football — up to the 19th century, the mass games were 'anything goes' affairs. A player could kick the ball or the man if it seemed necessary. It was equally acceptable to punch or carry the ball.

Mass football in London is mentioned by Fitz Stephen, who died in 1141, but it seems evident that it was played centuries before this. Even to this day the mass games survive in some places in Britain. At Jedburgh a mass game by the name of Fastern E'en Ba' is still played on the first Tuesday after the new moon following Candlemas, when the players are divided into two sides: the Uppies and Doonies, depending on the area in which they were born. It was played when William Hone was writing his *Every-Day Book* in the 1820s, and he describes the ball used as being made of leather with streamers attached. Hone suggests that this ball was meant to represent an Englishman's head. It is said to date back to the English occupation of Ferniherst Castle, on the outskirts of the town. The castle was stormed by the Scots and one of their number recognised an English officer who had raped his daughter. It was his head that is supposed to have been the first Jedburgh football. Still in Jedburgh, a similar game called Callants' Ba' is played by the youth of the town on Candlemas Day.

By the 18th century public opinion as well as that of the authorities was beginning to actively turn against Football. In 1796, after an inquest on a man who died by drowning in the river Darwent while engaged in a mass football game, the court put forward the following opinion:

A custom which, whilst it has no better recommendations for its continuance than its antiquity, is disgraceful to humanity and civilisation, subversive of good order and government and destructive of the morals, properties and very lives of the inhabitants.

Balls are not the only objects used in surviving mass games. There is, for instance the Haxey Hood Game in Leicestershire, in which tightly rolled lengths of sacking are used. There is, perhaps, something sinister about the ritualistic method of play, which it has been suggested could be symbolic of the struggle between winter and summer. However, the legend behind the game does not support this theory of the struggle between the seasons. It is said that sometime in the 13th century, while riding on the Isle of Axeholme, Lady Mowbray lost her hood. It was found and returned by 12 peasants from the village of Haxey. As a reward she gave to the village a piece of land, thence called the Hoodland, the rent from which had to be used to buy hoods each year to be played for by 12 villagers. The game is also thought to have been played at Epworth on the Isle of Axeholme.

On the Eve of St John (23 June) each year at Haxey a committee is elected consisting of 12 *Boggons* — sometimes called *Boggans* or *Boggins* — one *King Boggon* and a fool.

On the following day at 2 pm, to the pealing of the church bells, the committee meet dressed in scarlet jerkins and tall hats, except for the Fool who wears a grotesque costume; he has his face blacked and smeared with red ochre and is dressed in trousers of sackcloth with coloured patches and a red shirt. On his head he wears a tall hat with a goose's wing and red flowers adorning it. He carries a short-stocked whip on the end of which is a sock filled with bran. With this he belabours the bystanding folk as he passes. On this day the Fool is entitled to throw his arms around and kiss any women, even 'be she the highest in the land', and she must not show any resentment.

As a wand of office the King Boggon carries a bunch of willow strips. The Fool starts proceedings with a speech which ends with the words, 'hoose agen hoose, toone agen toone. If thou meets man, hook 'im down, but don't 'ut 'im'. As he is uttering these words some straw at his feet used to be set alight in a custom known as Smoking The Fool — this practice has been discontinued in recent years.

The boggons then go up to the top of Haxey Hill. There, on the village boundary, they form a circle with the King Boggon in the centre holding 13 hoods. The King Boggon throws a hood and if someone other than a Boggon catches it he tries to run to a nearby public house while the Boggons attempt to stop him. If he succeeds in reaching the pub he demands a shilling. If, on the other hand, he is caught by a Boggon, the hood is returned, to be thrown up again. On the 13th hood throwing, a part of the game known as the *sway* begins. Hundreds of people join in and attempt to force the hood into a public house. If successful, drinks on the house are called for and the hood is kept on the premises for the following year.

Leicestershire seems to be the home of the more strange mass games. In another game, casks are used instead of hoods. This is

71

the Hallaton-Medbourne Bottle Kicking, which takes place every Easter Monday at Hallaton. The game follows a scramble for pies, a custom said to date from Saxon times and an occasion when there was a bequest of a piece of land, the rent from which had to pay for 2 hare pies, a sufficiency of ale and 24 penny loaves to be scrambled for annually. In modern times veal or steak pies have been substituted.

Outside the village of Hallaton there is a hill called Hare Pie Bank, and it is here, early in the afternoon, that the pies are scrambled for. After this the bottle kicking begins. The Bottle Keeper, the master of ceremonies, has three bottles — which are in fact wooden casks. Two of these are filled with ale and the other, the second to be played, is empty. Each play starts with the Bottle Keeper dropping a cask three times and on the third drop the opposing teams of Hallaton and Medbourne try to kick or carry the casks over their village boundaries. The winning team, of course, keeps the ale.

In the early years of the 19th century schools were starting to take the game of Football seriously and to organise rules and styles. It was still a rough free-for-all; at Rugby School, for example, Football was a wild affair with up to three hundred players on the field. In this particular version of the game only kicks could be made forward, and only hand passes could be made to a player behind. In 1823 there was a landmark in the game at Rugby when, we are told, William Ellis (later the Reverend William Ellis) picked up the ball and, instead of kicking it forward or passing it to the rear, ran to the opponents' goal with the ball. Ellis may not have been the inventor of what we now call Rugby Football but he brought the game forward by a number of years.

Other schools developed their own rules and there was a multitude of variations. Generally speaking there were two basic forms of the game: the Dribblers (kickers) and the Handlers. The Dribbling game was taken up at Cambridge in 1855 and in Sheffield two years later, whereas the Handling code was adopted by the Blackheath Club in 1859 and by the Richmond Club in 1860.

What may be regarded as the forerunner of modern Soccer — played then with eight forwards — began in 1846 when the first set of Association Football rules were drawn up at Cambridge. But still there were no real standardised rules, the absence of which made inter-district matches difficult. In 1863 the Football Association was founded in an attempt to get all the factions together but it was several years before a set of standardised rules could be agreed.

72

Up to 1867 it was customary only to dribble the ball forwards, which made the game extremely slow and not a little boring. In that year the Football Association ruled that forward passing was allowed and this greatly increased the popularity of the game.

The 'Handling' game, as distinct from the 'Dribbling' game, was also making good progress, and in 1871 the Rugby Football Union was formed with standardised rules — this was and has remained the body governing the amateur game.

In Rugby Football there was an increasing need for the injection of professional players, particularly in the North of England. Players could not afford to take time off from work without payment or to be out of action because of injury. For this reason the Northern Rugby Football Union was founded in 1895, the clubs making payment to the players for loss of working time. This was not without considerable opposition from the amateur element and it did not become a fully professional game until three years later.

The Americans have never really taken to the Dribbling game of Soccer. American Football, as it is known today, has its roots in the mass games that spread to that side of the Atlantic in the 18th century, and the New World version was at least as brutal as the Old.

The football played in Australia originated as a kick-about and handling game in the Ballarat goldfields sometime around 1853 and it is believed there have been rules in existence as early as 1858. This was played 18 aside on a large oval ground, which could be anything between 120-170yds wide by 150-200yds long. The goals were strange in that they were marked by four posts in a row — two long and two short — the score depending upon between which posts the oval-shaped ball passed.

Gaelic Football was developed from the mass game. As with the game of Hurling, the rules were formulated at the time of the establishment of the Gaelic Athletic Association in 1884, under the patronage of the Archbishop of Cashel, Dr Thomas Croke.

For information on the football game of Karamoga, I am indebted to Major Douglas Harrison, late of the Kenya Police. It is called after the tribe from which the Police Ascaris are recruited. The game was played mainly in Uganda during the time when these territories were under the Union Jack. Karamoga is played on a field of roughly Association Football dimensions with goalposts, but this is where the resemblance ends — although it has been suggested that it was developed after seeing Association games played by the King's African

Rifles without the rules being known. There are nine players in each team and the game ends when a pre-agreed number of points have been scored. The points are scored, not in the conventional manner of driving the ball into the net, but by kicking the ball against the uprights which have black and white bands painted on them, more points being scored if the ball hits the top hand. It is played barefoot, but even so it is extremely rough, and injuries are numerous. There was, in fact, a semi-official *Karamoga-leave* in the Kenya Police, to facilitate recovery from injuries.

What must have been one of the strangest of all team ball games was one called Pushball, introduced in 1895 by the Newtown Athletic Club near Boston in the U.S.A. The ball was about 6ft in diameter and the game was played by teams of seven aside on a ground marked like an American Football ground, and played under similar rules. As far as can be ascertained, the game has now become extinct.

Basket Ball was invented by James A. Naismith, a Canadian who was working as a physical training teacher at the Y.M.C.A., Springfield, Massachusetts, in 1891. Naismith wanted a game to offset the flagging interest in free-standing exercises during the winter months. He nailed two peach baskets on a balcony, one at each end, at the Y.M.C.A. gymnasium, and the game of basket ball was born.

It would be interesting to know if Naismith was aware of a very old game played by South American Indians and called Ollamalitali (Pot-ta-Pok to the Maya Indians and Tichtli to the Aztecs). This game was played with a solid ball and the object was to get the ball through an elevated ring. This, it is believed, was an individual type of game and not a team game as basket ball. It is said that the winner was entitled to demand the clothing from all the spectators!

A mural in Tomb No.16 at Beni Hasan, Egypt, dated about 2000 BC, shows a representation of what appears to be two men in the hockey 'bully-off' position. Whether or not this depicts such a game is open to speculation. But this is not the only pictorial account found: in 1922 a bas-relief was discovered in Athens in a wall built by Themistocles (514-499 BC), with six men taking part in something that looks very like a Hockey match.

Certainly games played with sticks and a ball are very ancient and it is believed that there were several games of this type played at the time of the height of Rome.

It is thought that a kind of hockey game was played in

74

Lincolnshire in the 13th century. It seems likely that this was the game of English Bandy.

Most authorities agree that Hockey as it is known today descends from a mixture of Irish Hurling, Scottish Shinty, and Welsh and English Bandy, but the name itself probably originates from the Old French *hoquet,* meaning a crook.

The name Bandy comes from bent stick — *bandy legs* being an example of how the term has survived.

Bandy on Ice was particularly strong in the district of Bluntisham-cum-Earith, Huntingdonshire, and was certainly played there during the great frost of 1813-14. It was undoubtedly played before that time but there are no records. This was before the game of Ice Hockey, with its own rules, had been developed.

In Bandy, the 'cat' or 'kit' — the forerunner of the puck in Ice Hockey — was usually a ball but was sometimes a bung of cork or wood. The goal posts were at one time about 6ft apart but later the space was enlarged to 12ft — the idea being to prevent the goalkeeper from lying down on the ice to protect the goal.

In 1860 an attempt was made to introduce the game of Bandy into London, the Crystal Palace in December being the scene of the debut. After this, some London and Home Counties Cricket, Hockey and Rowing Clubs adopted Bandy as a winter activity.

By the end of the 19th century hockey had become more gentle, and women's hockey was becoming part of the sporting scene after growing up at the universities of Oxford, Cambridge and Dublin during the 1880s.

Irish Hurling is a game of considerable antiquity but it was only in 1884 that it was given standardised rules. With Gaelic Football, it is one of the toughest games now being played anywhere in the world.

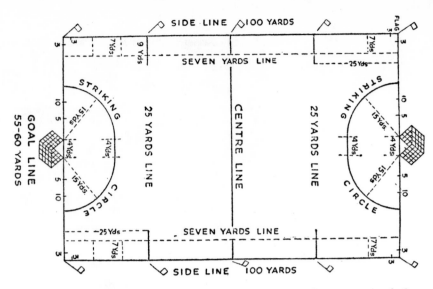

SIDE·LINE 100 YARDS

SEVEN YARDS LINE

GOAL LINE 55-60 YARDS

STRIKING CIRCLE

25 YARDS LINE

CENTRE LINE

25 YARDS LINE

STRIKING CIRCLE

SEVEN YARDS LINE

SIDE LINE 100 YARDS

Hockey Pitch

Scottish Shinty or Camanchd, is the ancient game of the Highlands, and is the intermediate between hockey and hurling. The game is played on a field between 140 and 250yds long and between 70 and 100yds wide. The goals at each end are called *hails* and are 12ft wide by 10ft high. Twelve players make up a team, each man carrying a *caman* — club with a triangular head. Bandy's descendant, ice hockey, probably originated around the 1860s at Kingston, Ontario, but there are other places that make claims for the game's invention. Wherever it was invented, it certainly achieved a great deal of popularity in Canada and the United States of America during the latter years of the 19th century.

In the 15th century, and probably before, the Iroquis Indians and other nations in the territory now known as Ontario and New York State, played a game called Baggataway. Sometimes this game was played to settle disputes and often hundreds of men took part over very large areas. Each man was armed with a long stick with a net at the end. After the settlement in Canada by the French, the game Lacrosse was developed from Baggataway, and was described by Catlin, who lived between 1793 and 1872.

Lacrosse was introduced into Britain from Canada in 1867 — in which year the rules were standardised — by a team of North American Indians on a demonstration tour, but it did not have an enthusiastic reception, and it was not until 1892 that the English Lacrosse Union was formed, the University and the Leys School, Cambridge, being the first to adopt the game.

It is thought that a ball game with the participants on horseback was played by the Persian kings in the Median period (c.600 BC), when it was known by the name of Chaugan.

The game was apparently not confined to males as the British Museum has a drawing of ladies playing Chaugan about the time of Akbar.

Brigadier J.R.C. Gammon tells me the game gradually spread eastward, probably along the great silk road north of the Hindu Kush and the Karkurrum Mountains to Afghanistan, India, Tibet, Kashmir and Bengal. It is also thought to have reached as far as China and Japan. The Byzantine Princes also knew the game in some form after a Tartar invasion about AD 700 as there are a large number of ancient Turkish miniatures in existence depicting such a game.

Stones, which could have been goal markers, have been found at each end of a 500yd pitch at Isfahan, Iran. These remains are believed to date from the 12th century. By that time

Larcrosse
1. Method of holding crosse in throwing with ball in position
2. Alternative method of throwing

the game was played over a wide area of the East and there is a widely accepted theory that the name 'Polo' originated from a Tibetian word, *pula* or *pulu*. The game was taken into North East India, in Manipur and Cachar, where it became a national game played in every village.

A minor expedition against Manipur in the mid-1800s, left some of the British troops in occupation whose officers in Manipur and tea planters of Cachar were soon playing regularly with the inhabitants. With Pig Sticking it became the universal sport of the British army in India. The Cachar Club, the oldest established Polo Club, was founded in 1859 and Major Sherar, RA, took a Manipuri team to play at Calcutta.

The Calcutta Polo Club which still exists was formed in 1862 and the game spread rapidly all over India in cantonments where soldiers were serving.

When imported into Britain, introduced by Captain Hartopp of the 10th Hussars, it was first played at Aldershot by his regiment versus the 9th Lancers in (according to Brigadier Gammon) 1871 — although the *Encyclopedia of Sport* (1898) gives this date as 1870. It is said that at this match the players used hockey sticks and billiard balls.

At Kabul, Afghanistan, the game of *Buzkashi* still survives. It is a game played on horseback by any number of players, on a field with no fixed boundaries. In the form in which it is now played, the horsemen, at full gallop, have to remove the carcass of a calf or a goat from a circular depression in the centre of the field, carry it around a marker at the end of the playing area and return it to the centre. It is said that in olden times a small boy was sacrificed for some ritualistic reason.

The game of Water Polo undoubtedly has its roots in the mass Football games, and its original names of Water Soccer, Football in Water, and Aquatic Handball are more appropriate than Polo. The game grew up in the 19th century at a time when swimming for pleasure was gaining ground. Official Water Polo rules were drawn up in 1880, and by 1896 there were fifty water polo clubs in Britain.

A game of mass Water Football is played each August Bank Holiday in the River Windrush at Bourton-on-the-Water, Gloucestershire. It is said that this annual game dates from the time of Richard II (1307-1327).

Handball games have been with us for a long time — just how long it is impossible to say, but we have plenty of evidence of such games in Roman times. One for children was called *Trigon*. As its name suggests, there were three players, each with a small ball made from wood or leather. They could throw it to either of the other two players, who had to punch it, or catch and throw it, thereby passing it on. Points were won or lost depending on whether the ball was caught or dropped. It was a game of agility, as often the three balls were in the air at the same time. Something similar is seen today in the children's games of King, Kingy and King Ball. At the museum at Corstopitum, Corbridge, Northumberland, there is a display of dodecahedron-shaped hollow balls, of the size and shape to be easily caught and it would seem possible that they were used in some game like Trigon. There was another Roman handball game played by men and boys in which a ball called a Follis was used. This was formed from an inflated bladder — indeed the name itself means windbag. Peter Moss, in his book *Sports and Pastimes through the Ages,* says that a similar game was played by European peasants throughout the Middle Ages.

We know there was a handball game played against the wall of the church at Badcary, Somerset, in 1765, and this may have been a hangover from an old and mysterious Eastertide custom of ballplay in the churches. Thomas Fosbroke (1777-1842) in his *Dictionary of Antiquities* writes about this Eastertide activity and ritual. Again, it is described in William Hone's *Every-Day Book* (1825). There was, it appears, a church Statute concerning the size of the ball to be used. The ball was received by the Dean who began the Easter Chant and, taking the ball in his left hand, began to dance to organ music. Around him danced the other clergy in a kind of ring-o'-roses hand-in-hand dance. The Dean threw the ball over the heads of the clergy and the choristers beyond the ring caught it and threw it back to the Dean.

The old French game of Palm-Play is part of the history of Tennis, Fives and Rackets. In the reign of Charles V (1337-80), it was fashionable to indulge in Palm-Play. The game consisted of receiving the ball and driving it back again with the palm of the hand. At first it was played with the naked hand, but later some players used to bind their hands with cords to make the ball rebound more forcibly, foreshadowing the tennis racket. The buildings used for Tennis were called Tripots and it was at one of these in 1427, called Le Petit Temple in the Rue Grenier, Saint Lazare, Paris, that a girl called Margot de Hainault played hand tennis with the naked palm and back of the hand better than any of the male players of the day.

Real (or Royal) Tennis was imported into England from France in the Middle Ages and was at once considered a suitable sporting indulgence for gentlemen. Acts were passed in 1388 and again in 1410 under which the playing of tennis by servants and labourers was prohibited on pain of six days' imprisonment. Henry VIII ordered the building of a tennis court at Hampton Court in 1530, and it was reconstructed by Charles II in 1660. Indoor courts consisted of a rectangle of about 100ft by 30ft bounded by a high wall. There were galleries jutting out from two short sides and one long side. On the long ungalleried side there was a buttress called a *tambour* running from floor to ceiling. Dividing the court into two equal halves there was a rope — forerunner of the net in modern Lawn Tennis.

The players wore felt slippers and special clothing, probably more fashionable than suitable for an energetic game. The balls were of white leather stuffed with dog's hair. The scoring

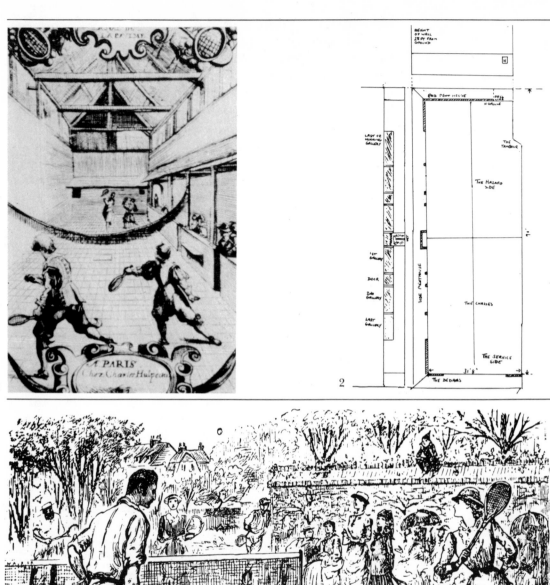

1. Early tennis print of 1632, showing the resemblance of early courts to a cloister
2. Early tennis court at Lord's, London
3. A game of Lawn Tennis in 1883

method was very unlike the lawn tennis scoring we know today and depended on how the ball was hit into and through the galleries. The points awarded were, however, similar to the present system: 15, 30, 40 (perhaps originally 45), Game. This is thought to be derived from the fact that the figure 60 had a significance in the Middle Ages as a whole number, much in the same way as 100 has today. Probably the origin is connected with the 60 seconds in one minute and 60 minutes in an hour.

The games of Fives and tennis were often confused in early references, and the name of Jeu de Paume seems to have been given to all games of this kind played with the hand. Tennis seems to have lost this name only after the introduction of the racket. Why Fives? It could be because we have five fingers on each hand and the use of these was a convenient method of scoring, or perhaps at some time five players were involved — but this seems unlikely. Another and more convincing theory is that the word may come from the French *fèves*, meaning beans. Perhaps the balls used in the early games were filled with beans. Even today, at infant schools, small children play with bags filled with beans as they are easier to catch.

There was, in the 18th and early part of the 19th centuries, a great entertainment centre to the north of London called Copenhagen House. Here many sports were played, including Fives, from about 1780, and one of the most famous players was one, John Cavanagh, who died in 1815 when the establishment was in its heyday. This court, and that at the Belvedere Gardens, attracted great crowds well into the middle of the 19th century. There were also lesser Five Courts at St Martins-in-the-Fields

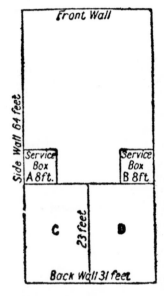

Rackets. Layout of court

Belvedere Gardens, Fives court

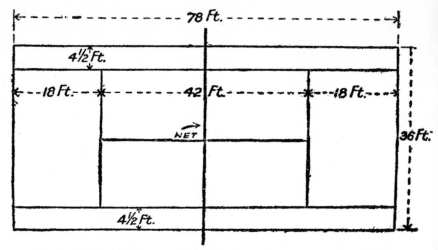

Tennis Court

Eton Fives

and at Leicester Fields. Fives also became the accepted exercise in the debtors' prisons, and we read that Dicken's Sam Weller watched Fives from a window in the Old Fleet Prison.

Fives became a Public School game in the early 1800s with variations in court design and methods of play in the several schools where it was played. Eton Fives was first recorded in

82

1825, when the game was played against the buttress on the wall of the Eton College Chapel. Eton Fives is the more usual form of the game played at other schools. The court is rectangular in plan — about 25ft long and 14ft broad. It is enclosed on three sides by thick walls coated with cement, the centre or front wall being 18ft high. On this there is marked a vertical line 3ft 8ins from the right hand wall, and on the left hand wall there is a low buttress called the 'pepper pot'. Eton Fives is always played as a doubles game.

Another game in this group is that of Rugby Fives, which dates from about 1850. Unlike the Eton game, Rugby Fives is played either as a singles or doubles game. A covered four-

Five-Ten Court

walled court is used. A variation of the Rugby game is played at Winchester and called, logically enough, Winchester Fives.

There was a rural form of Fives played in Yorkshire called Hoosey. The language of the game was one of dialect, with cries like 'two and tin to and an' on the fly'. The game began with a preliminary 'putting into t'hat', in which each player placed a small article from his pocket into a hat after which a neutral person, preferably a young child, drew out the articles two at a

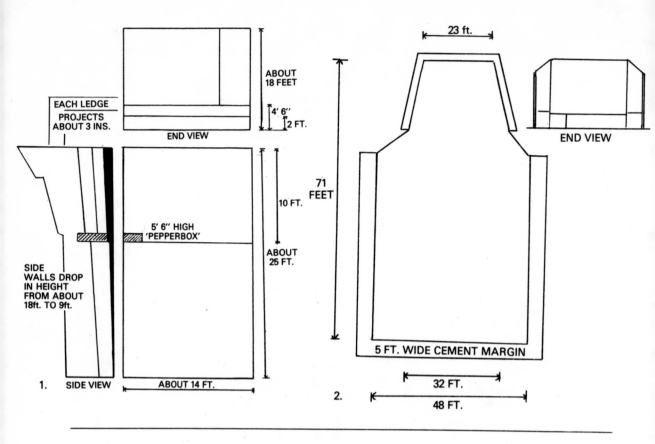

ABOUT 18 FEET

4' 6"

2 FT.

END VIEW

EACH LEDGE PROJECTS ABOUT 3 INS.

5' 6" HIGH 'PEPPERBOX'

SIDE WALLS DROP IN HEIGHT FROM ABOUT 18ft. TO 9ft.

1. SIDE VIEW

ABOUT 14 FT.

71 FEET

10 FT.

ABOUT 25 FT.

23 ft.

END VIEW

5 FT. WIDE CEMENT MARGIN

32 FT.

48 FT.

2.

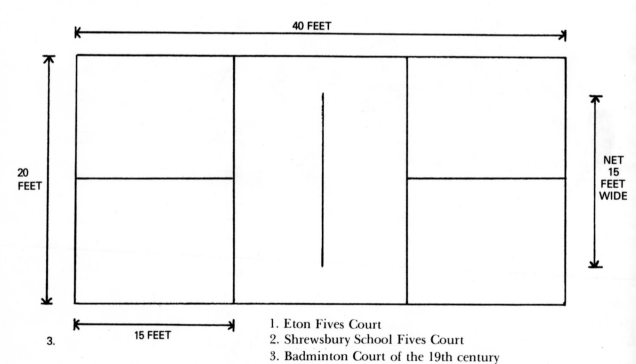

40 FEET

20 FEET

NET 15 FEET WIDE

15 FEET

3.

1. Eton Fives Court
2. Shrewsbury School Fives Court
3. Badminton Court of the 19th century

time, so selecting the opponents. The play consisted of hitting the ball against the side of a house or barn with the palm of the hand.

Hoose was another palm ball game, obviously related to Hoosey, which was played at Ampleforth College between the years 1887-92, according to contributions in *The Dalesman Magazine.* In this game the court was shaped in plan like a capital letter E with walls 15ft high. Two pairs of players competed at the same time on the court.

The Irish game of Handball or Caitch is a form of Fives on a court of about 60ft long and 28ft wide.

There was a Rackets open court at Westminster School before their new courts were built at the end of the 19th century. This game was played with a choice of balls, one type called *woodens* and the other *wires,* with trophies for each.

Rackets was played at Harrow School with a hard ball covered in white kid, by two or four players on an ashphalt or concrete enclosed court of about 62ft by 30ft. In this Harrow Game the 'front' wall has two horizontal lines: the *ply* line and the *service* or *cut* line. The Harrow Rackets game is claimed to have been played in the schoolyard in the 17th century.

Like many other games, Squash Rackets began in a completely fortuitous manner. We have no exact date, but it is believed that sometime in the middle of the 1800s, some boys were waiting to play rackets at the court of Harrow School, and began knocking up in the vacant space caused by the outside wall of the Rackets Court and the adjoining wall of one of the school houses. This knocking up became common practice and, either the noise of the hard ball on the walls, or perhaps the breaking of windows, caused the Housemaster concerned to protest and insist that if the boys were going to use this space for games, they must use a soft ball. The boys provided themselves with a soft ball and began the game of rackets played with a squashy ball. Squash, as it became known, caught on with the boys at the school to such an extent that they wanted to play it at home. Odd spaces at country houses were used for the game and, in time, special courts were built.

Something of a sporting revolution occurred in 1874 when Major Walter Clopton Winfield invented and patented a game called Sphairistike, played with pear-shaped, long-handled rackets and small rubber balls. The court was marked out on turf and was 30ft wide, tapering to 21ft at a 4ft high net with 5ft posts. The name given to the game may seem strange at first sight, but with *sphaira* meaning a ball, at least the root of the word is logical. The following year, 1875, Sphairistike was

Major W.C. Winfield

introduced at the British Croquet Championships at Lords Cricket Ground, by the M.C.C. as a form of light diversion. Later that year the M.C.C. issued a code of lawn tennis rules. Croquet had been, and was at that time, the great lawn game with an enormous following, but the new game took on immediately and, within a few years, had ousted Croquet.

Major Winfield's game was not without its enemies who derided Sphairistike by nick-naming it 'Sticky', but Lawn Tennis was here to stay, soon finding popularity abroad particularly in the U.S.A.

Towards the end of the 19th century an interesting combination of Lawn Tennis and Fives was introduced. At one end of the court there was a net arrangement called the *frame,* the lower portion of which is of netting and about the height of a Lawn Tennis net. The upper part is of wood in the centre of which and just above the netting, is a hole giving access to a box. The court itself could be of any size between 7 x 3½yds and 12 x 7yds. The object of the game is to serve the ball into the box but, if it rebounds off the wood, it is played by the opponent or opponents. This game, which never had any great popularity, was known by a number of names, including Five-Ten.

In 1895 there was an abortive attempt to introduce a game called Lawn Football. It was played with an Association football on a court 50ft long by 20ft wide, divided by a net, over which the ball could only be kicked or headed.

Pelota Vasca is said to be the fastest of all ball games. It originated in the Basque country and is now played in Spain, South America, and the United States, where it has gained considerable popularity. In Spain the game is also known as

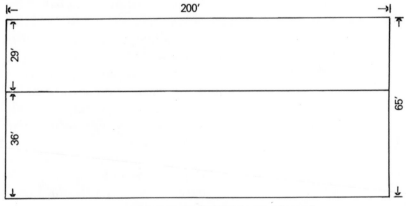

WALL AT EACH END OF COURT 36 FT. SQUARE
FLOOR OF CONCRETE.

Pelota Court

Pelota Basque and *El ble a'Cesta* — basket play. The *cesta* is a basket attached to the right hand and the game is played with a hard ball weighing about 4ozs, made from rubber and wire covered with leather. In play the ball is struck against two concrete walls set at right angles, known as the *fronton* and the *pared*. The court has a concrete floor 200ft by 65ft. There are usually four players — two on each side. The ball must always be in motion and never be allowed to touch the ground.

Although shuttlecocks were known to children as playthings in the Middle Ages, it took the Duke of Beaufort to introduce and popularise the game of Badminton, which he called after his house in Gloucestershire. Devised, it is said, to entertain his guests on wet days. In fact, he probably developed it from a game of Indian origin called Poona. At first small rubber balls were used when the game was played outside, and the shuttlecock was used only when the game was played indoors.

Finally, a mention of some lesser-known games that may only be included in a chapter concerned with the Tennis family.

Chin Lo is a highly skilful game from the East. In this the two players squat facing each other on the ground and toss between them a hollow ball made from open-woven strips of bamboo. The skill lies in the rule that only the feet may be used. In Burma, Chin Lo is played by a number of participants *standing* in a circle.

Like Chin Lo, the game of Talagang also comes from the East, in this case from West Pakistan. It again involves two players, each equipped with a short slat of wood. The object of the game is to toss another strip of wood from one to another, by using the slats only. The game is played very seriously and, like Chin Lo, requires a good deal of skill.

Graces it seems, is of European origin. In this case the object tossed is a hoop thrown and caught with the aid of one or two sticks held by each player.

Related to Graces was the outdoor court game of Ringral, which was introduced at Oxford, England in 1887. It was a game for two players on a court of any surface 78ft long with goals at each end 8ft high and 10ft wide. Each player had two short sticks with which he endeavoured to 'serve' a cane ring of about 7ins diameter into the opposite goal which the other player defended.

Typical of the pastimes of the 19th century was the game of Drawing Room Rackets which used the cups and balls — the development of the pastime of Bilboquet or cup and ball. The players had to throw the ball to each other, using only the cups.

4. Aiming Games

The relationship between bowling games, including Skittles, and Billiards, is so complex as to defy classification. Nor is it possible to chronologically relate the development of the games played today, for two reasons: we cannot be sure when a particular game emerged or to what extent the invention of each game was influenced by others existing at the time. We must think of the group of bowling games as a whole, try to establish their links with the others, and consider the areas or countries in which they have been played.

The name *marbles* is deceptive; only rarely are the various forms of the game played with balls made from real marble. However, the word is said to be derived from the Greek *marmaros* meaning to sparkle, and this may well indicate the place of the game's origin and perhaps the kind of material from which the early balls were made. We cannot tell. What we do know, or rather what tradition tells us, is that the children of Greece and Rome played games with nuts; flicking them into holes or a circle marked on the ground, or trying to knock the other nuts out of a circle or out of line. Aiming at a hole is still the object of a currently played game. Although there have been many variations of the game since Roman times, the idea has remained basically the same, and it surely must be one of the oldest surviving games. Rolling small balls into indented holes is a division of the Marbles family of games. One such game is called, Three Holes, each hole having its own value. Another, called Handers, employs a larger hole of about three inches across. It cannot be a coincidence that in the Kangra district, situated in the Himalayan foothills, a game is played involving flicking beans into a depression in the ground. This game has a very complicated system of scoring and it is thought to be ancient in origin.

Each year on Good Friday at Tinsley Green, Sussex, outside the Greyhound Hotel, the British Individual Marbles Championship is held. This contest has been a Sussex Inn game since the late 18th century, and tradition dates its origin to about the year 1600, when two villagers are said to have played the game to decide who was to have the hand in marriage of a local maiden. This explains why it is traditional

The game of Pell Mell

Quoits

89

The Game of
Skittles, c.1770

for men only to play marbles at Tinsley Green. A slab of raised concrete, called the *ring,* is covered with smooth damp sand. Forty-nine marbles are spread on the ring. These are little balls of baked clay of ½in diameter. Each player of the six man teams has his own *tolley,* which is again a ball of baked clay, but ¾in in diameter, and with these tolleys they attempt to knock out as many balls as possible.

There was a charming little ball game played by ladies in the 18th century, called Troule-In-Madam. It might rightly be associated with Marbles, although some authorities connect it with the Bagatelle family. It is played by rolling small metal or wooden balls into holes at the end of a bench. There was another version of the game called Trunks or Pigeon Holes, in which numbered arches took the place of the holes in the bench. German Balls was a marbles game which was also known as Die Shot or Marble Dice. In the game an eight-sided die, placed on a flattened ball, was used as a target for the marbles. These were rolled or flicked, according to the size used, and the number on the die when it came to rest was taken as the score.

Bowling, 13th
century

Bowling, 14th century

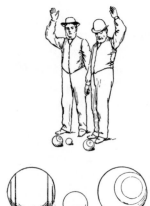

Bowls

Stone implements have been excavated in Egypt which suggest that a form of bowling was known in that part of the world as early as 5200 BC, and similar games are recorded in other parts of the world. In England, Bowls can be traced back at least to the 12th century. When William FitzStephen (died 1191), the biographer of Thomas Becket, refers to the youth of London taking their pleasure in *Jactu Lapidum*, it is thought that the allusion is to a game like the one we know as Bowls. According to a manuscript in the Royal Library at Windsor, the association known as the Southampton Town Bowling was formed in 1299. At that time Bowling and Skittling were one; there is a 13th-century illustration which shows men bowling at a cone, and it is believed that the two activities became separated only in the 16th century.

Both skittling and bowling have been banned by legislation from time to time. However, they have not suffered as much as many other forms of recreation at the hands of law-makers or the Church; even the Puritans, who prohibited almost every game, sport and custom, accepted bowls as a more or less harmless pursuit.

The Lewes Bowling Society in Sussex possesses a unique lime-tree-bordered green which was formerly the tilting ground of the Norman Castle. Just over three-quarters of an acre in area, the green is roughly the shape of a square with a triangle at one end. The surface has innumerable slight slopes, depressions and valleys. The cheese-shaped bowls have a considerably heavier bias than those used on other types of green, to combat the uneven ground.

Bowling, 14th century

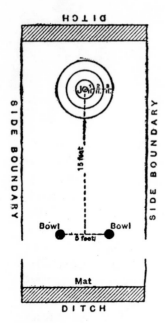

Bowls Green laid out
for drawing

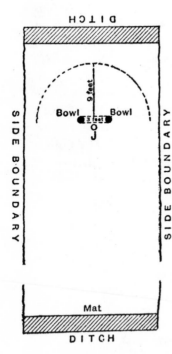

Bowls Green laid out
for trailing

Bowls currently takes two forms: the Flat Green, also called the Rink Game, and the Crown Green which, as its name suggests, is played on a raised green which falls gently to the boundaries. The Crown Green game, is played mainly in the North of England, the Midlands and Wales.

In the 19th century Bowling was at the height of its popularity, and a miniature form to play indoors was even devised called Parlour Bowls or German Bowls.

Petanque or Boules is a French game of Bowls. It is usually played on an earthy surface, devoid of grass, and involves the throwing of heavy metal balls. The marker ball (or *jack* as it is called in the English game) is named *cochonnet* meaning little pig. Some authorities suggest that this game is of English origin and was, in fact, the game Sir Francis Drake was playing when the coming of the Armada was brought to his notice. It is impossible to confirm or deny this suggestion.

Irish Bowling was played on the roads of Ireland with heavy metal balls, the object being to bowl the ball as far as possible. Distances of half a mile were not exceptional. Needless to say, the game has lost popularity with the increase in motor traffic.

To go back to an even more primitive form of bowling, there was, up to the close of the 19th century, an old Servian game in which five stones were built up in the form of a pyramid; another stone was aimed at this with the object of scattering the five stones as far as possible.

There have been a number of theories put forward on the origin of Skittles. One of the most widely held is that the skittles themselves were first used in Germany during the 3rd century AD, when peasants carried flat-bottomed clubs for throwing when hunting and in defence. The Christian monks, it is said, found these clubs a convenient method of teaching religion, by setting them up in certain formations to represent various temptations. Balls or stones were rolled at the clubs to knock them down, symbolic of overcoming the temptations. In time, the instruction became a recreation. On the other hand, the Scandinavian word *skyttel*, meaning to shoot, must have some connection with these objects.

Skittles were probably known in Britain before the Norman invasion. However, through the Middle Ages they were known as *kails*, or *kayles* in England and *kyles* in Scotland. These names were a corruption of the French *quilles*, meaning peg, which suggests that the use of them in games became more widespread after 1066. There is an alternative: the word could come from the Old German *kegil* or *chegil*, meaning a cone-

shaped object. This would support the theory of the German origin of Skittles.

In the reign of Edward III (1327-77) attempts were made to restrain Skittles and Bowls as they were not considered aggressive or warlike enough for the times. In 1541 a law was passed forbidding the keeping of a bowling alley for 'gain, lucre, or living' and that 'no manner of artificer or craftsman of any handicraft or occupation, husbandman, apprentice, labourer, servant at husbandry, journeyman or servant of artificer, mariner, fisherman, waterman or any serving man should play bowls except in the twelve days of Christmas'. The object of this ordinance was to promote greater interest in Archery. This and other similar Acts were not repealed until the year 1845, but they had, of course, fallen into disuse by then.

By the time of the Stuarts, Bowls and Skittles had become two separate games and the latter was discouraged, as skittle alleys were alleged to be, and doubtless were, 'places where money, sense and curses were thrown away'. Throughout the ages the most popular number of skittles in the game has been nine, but as many as fifteen have been used in some variations. Kayles, the game that carried the early name for Skittles, was played at festivals in the Middle Ages. In this game a set of six or eight conical pins was set up in a straight line. The player stood about 5yds away and had to knock down the pins by throwing sticks. When a ball was rolled at the pins instead of the stick being thrown, the game was called Closh.

Long Alley is one of the more ancient forms of Skittles which survives mainly in Nottinghamshire and North Leicestershire, and is said to date back to the 12th century. The pitch, which is

Kayles, 14th century

93

under cover and specially built, is 12yds long and 2yds wide on a floor of slate or boards. There are nine pins, conical-shaped and 13ins high, except for the 'king pin' which is taller. The missiles, called 'cheeses', are small round-ended logs, weighing 3-4lbs.

Ring Skittles was a variation on the basic theme. It was played in the North of England during the Middle Ages, using twelve pins set in a circle. The missiles were wooden balls, sliced in half; these were bowled the length of the alley and had to circle the pins before knocking any over.

Old English Skittles is the form of the game played in London. It was enormously popular up to the 19th century when the card and table billiard games became fashionable, causing the skittles game to fade. It can still be found in some taverns and inns, played on a 21ft pitch called a 'run'. The pins, of which there are nine, are made from hornbeam and are about 15ins high. The *cheeses* are actually balls, biased on one side, and weighing up to 12lbs.

Western Skittles, as its name suggests, is most popular in Devon, Cornwall and Somerset. It is thought to have been developed in the 17th century, when it was played on earthern pitches; these are now made of wood or concrete, are 2yds wide and between 9yds and 13yds in length. In some cases the pitch is cambered, but more often it is flat. Western Skittles is a game which varies in detail from place to place. The nine pins are usually about 10ins high with a larger king pin, either in the middle or at the front of the formation. The balls are about 5lbs in weight.

Dutch Pins was a game using nine pins and a narrow pitch, similar to Long Alley. In this game the king pin has to be knocked down first before scoring can begin. It was played extensively in America in the 19th century by Dutch settlers. Was this the game, the noise of which, when played by giants, awoke Rip Van Winkle? In 1845 the game was declared illegal because of the rowdiness and brawling that went on at the alleys. The clever operators evaded the law by adding a tenth pin and positioning the skittles in a triangular formation instead of the usual diamond. Ten Pin Bowling was born — a moment that led to the formation of the American Bowling Congress in 1895. However, Ten Pin Bowling was not new. It is believed that there was a ten-pin game in Suffolk in the 17th century which resulted in a 19th century game called Kockemdowns, using a centre king pin.

Of all the green games — those played on grass and lawns — none have ever had the popularity of Croquet; at the height of

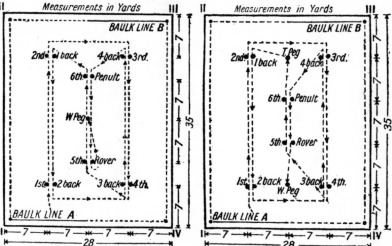

Croquet. Position of hoops and course of play in the two methods of playing the game.

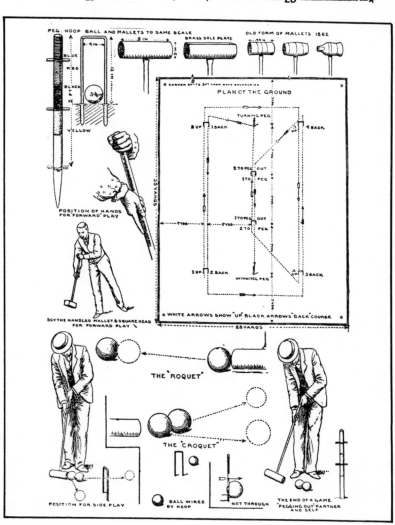

The game of Croquet

Ancient Lawn
Billiards

its reign it outshone even Lawn Tennis as it is known today. The game probably takes its name from the French *croc*, meaning a hook. It has been suggested that shepherds played the game with their crooks. The game known in Britain in the 19th century was almost certainly a French export — Maurice B. Reckitt, who played tournament croquet in 1905, and who became President of the Croquet Association, believes that British tourists saw it played by peasants on hard sands in Brittany in the 1850s. There are some reports of croquet being played in Ireland in 1847, and there are some authorities who contend that the game may even have originated in that country. Croquet became something of a craze and hardly a house with a lawn was without its croquet set. However, after Major Winfield invented and introduced his lawn tennis game of Sphairistike in 1874 (see page 85), the game began to decline and almost disappeared. It is ironic that Sphairistike was first shown to the public at the National Croquet Championships.

In the thirty years when croquet was king of the lawn games, several indoor versions were available commercially: Carpet Croquet, Parlour Croquet and Table Croquet. These were all similar but with different sized balls and hoops.

During the Middle Ages there was a form of lawn bowling which may or may not have been a forerunner of croquet. This is thought to have been played on the knees. In this position one had to push balls through hoops. This may have been the game calted Billyards which is recorded as being played at fairs and revels during the Middle Ages. There seem to be no details available of this game, but the similarity of the words must suggest that it was a ground version of the early table game of Billiards, using a king pin.

That Billiards is a development of the lawn game of Bowls, there can be little doubt. The name itself does not give much of an indication as to how it evolved; all that can be said is that it comes from a French word meaning ball, and there are references to the game of Ballyards possibly an alternative spelling to the croquet-like game. It is hard to believe that it is a

97

Billiards

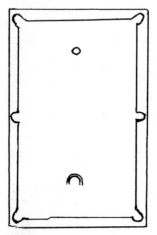

Probable layout of
Billiard Table in
1674, showing
positions of Post and
King

game of solely French origin. A French writer, Bouillet, in *Academie des Jeux,* ascribes the invention of Billiards to the English. On the other hand, according to Reilly's English translation of the Abbe McGeoghelar's *History of Ireland,* there is a reference to Billiards in the will of Cathire More, a sub-king of Ireland, who died in the early part of the 2nd century. We have a mention, but only a mention, of billiards by Edward Spencer in 1591, and early in the 17th century James I ordered a '*Billiarde Bourde,* twelve foote broade, the frame being walnutte'.

Billiards was described more precisely by Cotton in his *Compleat Gamester* (1674) as being played with two white balls and heavy curved sticks made from Brazil wood or Lignum Vitae, one end thicker than the other, called *maces.* We also know from prints that the 17th century billiards was played on a rectangular table covered with cloth over a wooden board, with six pockets. At one end of the table was a metal peg called the king — hence the expression 'king pin'. A hoop called the bridge was placed at the other end. Each player had an ivory ball and a mace. Scores were kept by a complicated system of points: for instance, if a player could touch the king with the ball without knocking it over, one point was scored. Knocking over the king or putting one's own ball into a pocket lost one point. The duration of the game depended on whether it was played in daylight or by candlelight; five points up in the case

Cannonade or Castle
Bagatelle

German Billiards

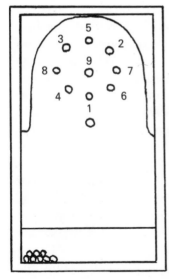

Bagatelle Table

of the former and three points only if artificial light was used. The third ball, coloured red and called the caramboler or rover, was introduced in the 18th century, as were the tipped and tapered cues.

Trucks was a game played in the 17th century and took the form of a greatly enlarged variety of Billiards. It was played on a long table with twenty-six pockets, three on each of the short sides and ten on each of the long sides. The king and the bridge were called the sprigg and arglio respectively, and were solidly fixed into the table. The balls were about the size of tennis balls and the iron-tipped maces used made it a very noisy game.

The first public Billiard Room in England was the Piazza in Covent Garden, which was opened in the early 19th century at a time when the modern billiards game was developing. Billiards was the subject of some legislative attack: the Gaming Act of 1845 forbade the licensees of taverns and alehouses to allow the game of Billiards on Sundays, Christmas Day and Good Friday. Around this period the slate-bedded table was replacing the old wooden-based table; the first recorded slate-bed table was one made by John Thurston in 1834 and delivered to White's Club in St James's Street, London. The number of balls used was standardised at three instead of two or four. The rubber cushions around the table came into use about 1838 — again the invention of John Thurston.

Snooker was born in an Indian Army mess in Jubbelpore in 1875, invented by Colonel Sir Neville Chamberlain — the dashing leader of Indian Irregular Horse. Originally it was meant as little more than a joke but, as often happens with jokes, it was taken seriously and when it was brought to England in 1885 it quickly spread throughout the country. The word *snooker* originated at the Royal Military Academy where it was used as a slang term for a young army cadet. The game is sometimes referred to as Slosh.

Bagatelle broke away from the bowling-billiards mainstream when sometime in the 17th century, possibly in France, someone had the idea of playing on a table with numbered holes set in the surface. Tables were anything from 6ft to 10ft long and 1ft 6ins to 3ft wide. In time pins, arches and bells were added, and various names were given to the games according to the arrangement of these hazards: German Billiards, Russian Bagatelle, Sans Egal, Irish Cannon Game, and Mississippi.

During the 19th century a number of games on the bagatelle theme were evolved using miniature tables of both rectangular and other shapes. One of these was called Cannonade, Bombardment or Castle Bagatelle, which was played on a

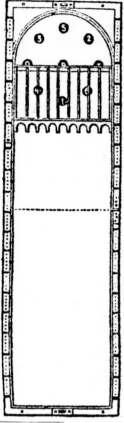

Mississippi Bagatelle

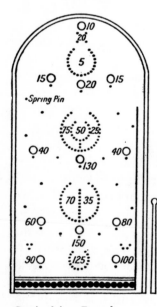

Corinthian Board

round enclosed table with a number of small balls and a teetotum. This was spun to knock the balls into small pockets. In some cases the balls knocked over small castles which were protected from the teetotum by hoops.

There is a tradition that 'Auld Daddy Scotland' received the gift of Curling from Albyn Jove, who gave it as he sat one day 'bare leggit on a snawy brae icicles at his snoat' and crying:

> O! for a cheery heartsome game
> To send through a' the soul aflame,
> Pitt birr and smeddum in the frame
> And get the blude a-dingling!

The Reverend John Ramsey was the first to write an account of Curling, in 1811. He said it was of continental origin, and since then many historians have declared it to be a Dutch invention of the 15th or 16th century. But another clergyman, the Reverend John Kerr, writing in the *Badminton Library* on ice sports, said there is no trace of the game in the Low Countries, and the etymology of the terms used does not prove its continental origin. The Dutch, however, did have a game called Kluyten, or Kalluyten, played on ice, and this game was mentioned in Killian's *Etymologican Teutonicas* in 1632.

Whatever its origin, Curling arrived in Scotland, the first known club being formed at Kilsyth near Glasgow in 1510, and there are some ancient Curling stones dated 1511 to be seen at the Macfarlane Museum, Stirling. Some authorities claim that Curling is even more ancient in Scotland and that the reason why the Scottish Parliament's Act of 1457 prohibiting Golf and Football made no mention of Curling is that the use of heavy stones could be considered a valuable war-like exercise and therefore one to be encouraged.

There is reason to believe that in its early form Curling was a kind of ice quoits played with stones. The terms, *coiting*, *kuting*, and *quiting* have all been used when describing the game of Curling; but in its traceable history it has grown far away from quoits.

Writing in 1848, Professor Ferguson, reports seeing in Bavaria an ice game which had at least a superficial resemblance to Curling. The game was played on a rink of about 50yds in length, using moveable wooden tees and 'sticks' with 25lb weights on the end. These 'sticks', with handles of about 9ins ran on 'soles' about 1ft diameter.

The game we know as Shove Ha'penny has certainly been played in various ways as a tavern activity since Tudor times and is a development of the earlier Shuffleboard. In the

Museum of Roman Antiquities at York there are some discs with domed upper surfaces, which look as if they could have been used on a shuffleboard, but this is sheer speculation and there is no evidence that the game was played in Roman times. The first reference we have of the game is a royal one; the Privy Purse in 1532 records that in January, 'Lord William won nine pounds of the King at Shoville Bourde'.

The shuffleboard was often 10yds long and the discs must have been very large and heavy. Joseph Strutt, in the early 19th century, records seeing a board in a 'low public house in Benjamin Street, near Camberwell Green, which was about 3ft wide and 39ft 2ins long'. This, it was claimed, was the largest board in London. The idea in shuffleboard was to land the disc over the edge of the table without it falling off. There were also two lines marked across the table, and if the discs passed over these, a score was still made — probably one point over the first line, two over the second, and three for resting on the edge. A miniature version of Shuffleboard was first called Shove Groat

Curling with a
threatening storm

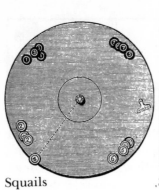

Squails

Summer Ice

or Shoffe Grotte. The boards used in this game were almost identical to those on which Shove Ha'penny is played today. Sometimes they were scratched or chalked on tavern tables but more often they were specially made from slate or hardwood, slate boards being particularly popular in Hampshire.

Played only in a small area of Dorset, around Swanage, is the game of Swanage Board. It is similar in principle to Shove Ha'penny in so far as the disc has to be skidded along the table to stop at a given distance. Traditionally, five Guernsey pennies should be used but sometimes these are replaced by Irish halfpennies. The board is about 4ft 6ins long and 1ft wide.

Squails or Trails was a Victorian game related to Shove Ha'penny, played on a circular table in the centre of which was a raised boss with a ring marked around it. The object was to get as many discs, called *squails,* as possible into the ring and to knock out those of the other players.

The Indian game of Carrom has some features which show a family resemblance to Shove Ha'penny, although it is considered by some people to be more allied to Billiards. It has been played in India since about 1885. Carrom is played on a 29ins square board, polished with boric powder, with a hole at each corner, with eighteen flat counters, the size of the pieces used in draughts. These *carromen* are placed at the centre of the board in a regular pattern around a single red counter called the *queen.* The object of the game is to pot one's own counters into the corner pockets by flicking another similar-sized *carroman* from behind the baseline with the thumb and forefinger. The baselines are made by a square marked approximately 3ins within the edges of the board.

Hopscotch is one of the oldest of children's games and, it is thought, was probably played in Rome. Areas are marked on the ground in a pattern, which varies according to the part of the country in which the game is being played. The object of this game is to hop on one foot and push the 'hitchidobber' into

102

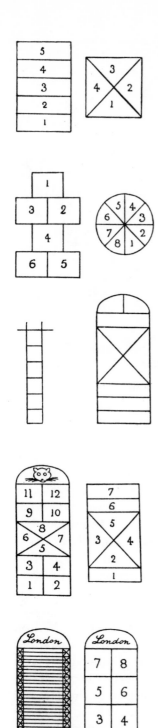

Hopscotch variations

each square in sequence. The 'dobber' can be any disc-shaped object: a stone or even the base of a broken bottle. The name Hopscotch is unlikely to owe its origin to Scotland. 'Scotch' is from the word meaning to trace, so we get 'tracing with a hop'.

Pitching or throwing of a stick, stone or ball at a target from a stationary position is one of the elementary forms of a game. In its simplest form, it can be seen when children set up a tin can on a wall and knock it off. It typifies an idling or contemplative pastime. Who has not sat on a pebble beach and thrown stones at a breakwater post? The group of pitching games is closely allied to that which includes bowling and skittles, but the element of height is added.

Loggats was a game played at fairs and other merrymakings. It consisted simply of throwing a club-like stick at a post. The word is probably an extension of *log*, a piece of wood. It is said that the traditional prize for Loggats at sheep-shearing festivals was a black fleece, presented to the winner by the farmer's maidservant. It was the custom for the girl to kneel on the fleece and be kissed by all the men present.

The game of Loggats must surely be connected with that of Aunt Sally ('Sally' probably derived from the French, *saillir*, meaning to stick out), which is still popular in some Oxford public houses. Timothy Finn in *The Watney Book of Pub Games* suggests that Aunt Sally is probably of 17th century origin when it might have been played by Royalist soldiers. Finn also suggests that it may have a relationship with the very much earlier tournament activity of Riding at the Quintain and Tilting at the Ring. Personally I disagree with this theory and believe it is an adaptation of Loggats.

The pitch, which can be either in or out of doors, is 11yds in length. At the end there is an 'iron', which is a tube driven into the ground to stand 3ft high, with a small platform on the top. On this stands a 'dolly'; simply a piece of wood. The object is to knock the dolly from the platform. To do this the players, who can be in teams of up to eight in number, throw six sticks each. Strikes on the dolly are called 'crosses', and misses are called 'blobs'.

Wallops was a game involving pitching at skittles, played in Wensleydale, Yorkshire. All the equipment for the game was made locally and consisted of nine pieces of wood each about 8ins long, 2ins thick, and sharpened at one end. The throwing sticks were about 2ft long and 2ins thick. The Wallops, or pins, were placed on a hard surface in three rows of three each, with slightly more than the length of the throwing stick between them. The throwing distance was 9yds for men and 6yds for

Aunt Sally at a
fashionable party

women. To knock down seven wallops from the nine was a considerable feat.

Over the years there have been many games involving pitching on a table, and one of these, called Daddlums, was played throughout the eastern and south-eastern counties of England. The name is said to have been derived from a word in use in the 13th and 14th centuries, which might well give a clue to its time of origin, even if the meaning of the word itself has been lost. Daddlums was played on a narrow table about 18ft long with a low wall on three sides — open at the players' end. The pitching mark was 8-10ft in front of the table. The missiles were small discs called cheeses which were thrown at nine small pins at the other end of the table.

The game of Hood Skittles was, and to a limited extent still is, played in parts of the East Midlands, such as Melton Mowbray and Northampton. Like other games which make use of skittles, it is said to have originated in the Middle Ages. Hood Skittles is played on a long, low, leather-covered wooden table at one end of which are stood the nine pins in a diamond formation. Over this there is a leather hood. The missiles are small leather padded 'cheeses' thrown from about 9ft in front of the table.

Devil among the Tailors, also known as Table Skittles and Skittles Board, is a compact form of nine pins. The name originates from the saying, 'nine devils make one tailor',

104

inspired in 1783, when the London tailors rioted in protest against a defamatory play called *The Tailors — A Tragedy for Warm Weather*. In this game may be detected elements from Skittle Alley, Ringing the Bull and even the ritualistic maypole, all of which may or may not have had something to do with its conception, which is thought to have occurred sometime in the 15th century.

The equipment consisted of a large wooden tray in which stood a small box, upon which there were nine wooden pins. On one side of the tray there was a post about 3ft high; to the top of this was attached a cord carrying a small wooden ball, which was swung round to knock down the pins. There is a legend in the West Country of a man who could swing the ball through the pins without knocking any over, meet the ball with the sole of his foot and send it back again to remove a match placed on top of one of the pins.

Couplette, a miniature form of Devil Among the Tailors, using small balls instead of pins, was a children's game in the 19th century. It consisted of a board with nine recesses to take the nine balls, and on the corner of this board was a post with a suspended ball similar to that in the parent game.

Which came first — the game of Quoits or that of Pitching Horseshoes? Both are virtually the same game, and the issue would seem to be the question of manufacture; were iron rings specially wrought to play the game, or were the existing products, horseshoes, utilised? Personally I think both styles of game were developed together and grew up side by side, with special rings made if a smith's time and services were available,. or with horseshoes if circumstances and locality prevented the use of quoits. When armies were engaged in war, the soldiers would hardly want to carry heavy quoits around and would use horseshoes in their recreation.

There is an interesting theory in regard to the origin of the Quoits game. The Sikhs of India used sharp throwing rings as hunting and fighting weapons, and it is supposed that demonstrations of these were given in Roman arenas. It is possible, therefore, that the game of Quoits came from this source.

The game in one form or another has certainly been played at festivals since the Middle Ages, and it was also a tavern and village green activity, reaching a peak in Georgian times. Since the last century there has been a steady decline in Britain and the game now survives in an organised form only in small pockets throughout the country, mainly in the northern counties.

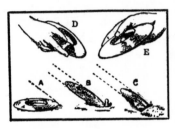

Quoits
A. Ringed quoit
B. A cutter
C. A quoit pitched true
D & E. Holds

I am indebted to Mr Oliver Nichol, an ex-champion quoits player from Prudhoe, Northumberland, for details of the two forms of the game: the Clay Pitch and the Grass Pitch games. In both cases the pitch is 10yds long between the two pins, called 'hobs', iron posts driven into the ground so they stand up for 2ins when in clay and rather more for grass ends — the areas round the hobs. (*British Rural Sports* by Stonehenge (1875) gives the distance between the hobs as 19yds). The quoits used are cast-iron rings weighing 6½lbs for use on clay ends and 4lbs for grass ends. The two types are also slightly different in shape, but both have the raised upper surface called the 'hill' the lower surface is concave and called the 'hole'. Usually teams consist of two or four players, who take alternate throws. The object is to get all the quoits of one's own team on a hob and to exclude those of the other team. Points are scored depending upon where the quoits fall: 2 points for a 'ringer' and 1 point for the quoit nearest the hob. The game ends when the score of one team reaches 21 or, in some cases, 41 points.

Penny Prick was the name of the medieval game of the Quoits family in which a coin had to be knocked off a peg in the ground. A poem of 1616 reads:

> Their idle houres (I meane all houres beside
> Their houres to eat, to drinke, drab, sleepe and ride)
> They spend at Shove-boord, or at Penny Pricke.

The theme of Penny Pricke is carried on in the game of Brasses. The first indication I had that such a game existed came in the King William Hotel, a dummy pub in that remarkable and spectacular mock-up street, called Half Moon Court, in the Debtors' Prison Museum, York. I understand the pub once stood in a street near York Minster. In the King William there is a glass-fronted case containing nine dome-topped discs of about 4½ins diameter. One is unmarked while the others have punched indents from one to eight. By the side of this case hangs a trophy shield carrying dates from 1914 to 1919 and inscribed 'Brasses — Working Mens' Club Union Limited'. After some enquiries it was found that the game was still played around the Whitby district. The method of play is similar to that of Quoits, with a clay-ended pitch of 10yds. A penny is placed on each hob, and knocking this off constitutes a 'hobber'. The brasses are thrown so that they *edge* themselves into the clay and do not bounce away from the hob.

Caves is a Suffolk game of bar quoits and many taverns between Sudbury and Thetford have their Caves Board used as much as the universal Darts. The board is round, about 12ins diameter, with five holes cut in it to receive the rubber ring quoits; these holes are numbered from 1 to 5. The board is set at an angle and the quoits are thrown from about 9ft away.

Cork Flicking was a tavern game which once had an appeal in northern counties of England. The corks were flicked with the thumb either at a target or into a depression cut in a board standing at an angle against a wall.

Deck Quoits is a shipboard game using rings of rope on a court which is double-ended, each end having a target area similar to an archery target. The rings are thrown from one end to land on the target area at the other. The game is played either as singles or as doubles. This is a game that goes back many years as a seafarers' game, certainly to the days of Nelson, but probably the original of shipboard quoits game is Bucket Quoits — using a bucket instead of a marked target area.

Dobbers is a West Midland game resembling Quoits. An 18ins square board is used, within which there are two circles and a central iron peg. The missiles are four flat rings, black on one side and white on the other, and to score they must land with the black side uppermost. The rings are thrown from a 10ft mark and the scores are five points for a ringer, two points for an inner circle and one point for the outer circle.

A fairly widespread throwing game in the southern half of England is Dunks, Dumps, or Toad in the Hole. These are the names given to the game when played in Sussex public houses, and in this version the equipment consists of a wooden box standing on legs of about 3ft in height. The top of the box, about 18ins square, is angled towards the players and has a covering of lead. In the middle there is a hole, just large enough to receive a disc or token made from brass or lead. Players stand about 9ft from the box and throw the token so that it stays on the top or, more desirably, falls through the hole into a drawer below. Sometimes the top of the box is cambered, but more often it is flat. The players try to *edge* the tokens so that they bite into the lead and fall flat rather than bounce off. Two points are awarded for a 'hole' and one point if the token remains on the top of the box.

Tossing the Penny, or Penny in the Hole, is the East Anglian version of Toad in the Hole in which the heavy old George II and George III pennies are used to this day. Often the hole in the top of the box is of a semi-circular shape.

In Spain there is a game with an obvious relationship to this family of games. It is called Juego de la Rana — the Game of Frog. It is played on a table of about 2ft square, enclosed by walls on three sides. In this enclosed area there are several openings into which the cast iron discs must enter in order to score. There are five open holes which each score 5 points; two holes covered by arches which score 10 points; a revolving wheel into which the disc must be thrown to score 25 points; a cast iron frog, the open mouth of which scores 50 points; in the back wall there are three slots which score 75, 80 and 100 — the last being the lowest slot. Ten discs, each about 1½ins diameter, are thrown from 10-13ft in front of the table.

Another game that must be considered in the same section as Quoits is the tavern activity of Ringing the Bull, Baiting the Bull, or Bullring. It is reputed that the game has been played for the past 800 years at the Trip to Jerusalem, a tavern carved out of the rock outside Nottingham Castle. One can only speculate on the origin of the game. It could well have been devised by farm workers in idle moments; a bull's nose ring being aimed at a hook in a barn beam. There is no formal standardised method of play and the game varies from place to place, depending on the space available and the height of the room. A hook is screwed into the wall or into the nose of a stuffed bull's head. From the ceiling, and about 6ft from the bull, is suspended a cord at the end of which there is a ring. The player has to swing the ring so that it falls over the hook.

Brother Jonathan is a game of throwing coins or discs on to a board marked with numbered areas, the larger areas having low numbers. The score is the sum of all the numbers in which a coin lands without touching a line. Not unlike Brother Jonathan is the old shipboard game of Bull Board which is played on a board about 1½yds square and tilted towards the players. This is marked with squares numbered from 1 to 10 or from 10 to 100; it also has the letter 'B', or the head of a bull, in areas at the sides of the board. The missiles used to be leather-covered lead rings about the size of a half-crown; more recently they have taken the form of small sand-filled pads or bags. Before scoring a player has to score a 'B' or a bull at each turn. A later version involves starting on the figure 1 and working through the numbers until the 10 is reached, then on to a 'B' and then in reverse order of the numbers.

The children's game of Tiddlywinks falls into this class of activity as the missile is projected from a stationary position. One cannot start to speculate on the origin of Tiddlywinks but there are many surviving bone discs of considerable antiquity. Worthy of mention is the charming accessory of the game made in Victorian times: the Tiddlywinks Tower. This was a miniature bell tower made from either tin plate or wood. The object was to flick the tiddlywink into one of the window openings and so ring the bell.

If croquet was derived from bowls, as I believe, then somewhere there is a branch line from the family tree which led to Pell Mell and — dare I say it — Golf. Some authorities contend that Pell Mell is on a direct line of descent between bowls and croquet, but I cannot subscribe to this theory. The fact that the ball has to be lifted from the ground in Pell Mell to score takes it away from the direct line of bowls, skittles, billiards and croquet, and makes it a far closer relation to golf.

Pell Mell may have had an ancestor in the form of a Roman game in which the players are believed to have struck at leather balls, aiming at trees with curved sticks. Another support for the golf relationship theory?

Pell Mell came to England from the mainland of Europe in the 17th century. It was played on a level court of sand, covered with powdered cockle shells in the centre of which was erected a kind of gibbet suspending a metal ring about 1in diameter. Two types of ball were used: a heavy wooden ball for driving off and a smaller metal ball for playing through the ring. Charles II introduced the game from Flanders, where it was called *Le Jeu de Mail*. The king had his Pell Mell court built at St James's Park and, of course, the road Pall Mall takes its name from that court. Samuel Pepys records seeing it played there by the Duke of York in 1661. Mallets and other implements used in the game were found in a house being demolished in 1845 and are now in the British Museum. The length of Pall Mall is typical of the Pell Mell courts which were often up to half a mile long and surrounded by high walls.

A form of the game survives to this day. This is a game called Mell and, as far as I know, can be found in only one place: at the Freemason's Arms, Hampstead, where there is an active Lawn Billiards and Skittle Club. The Mell court is circular, about 40ft diameter, the outer ring consisting of fine gravel; the apron, which is a projection from the centre circle, is made from wood blocks. The players have four balls each and the object is to play the balls through a ring which stands on a pedestal in the centre of the circle. The balls are 8lbs in weight and they have to be lifted by means of a cue which has an iron loop at the end.

The earliest reference to Golf dates from 1457, when the Scottish Parliament prohibited it, probably because it was thought to be a pastime too peaceful to provide good practice for war. Joseph Strutt considered Bandy Ball to be an ancestor of golf; in this game, curved sticks are used to hit a ball over a wide area.

Whatever its origin, the game was introduced to England from Scotland when it was brought to the court by James I (James VI of Scotland), although it was not received with much enthusiasm. Indeed golf in Scotland had organised support earlier than most games. The Gentlemen Golfers (now called the Honourable Company of Edinburgh Golfers) was formed at Leith in 1744, and ten years later came the most famous of all clubs, the Society of St Andrews Golfers which, in 1834, became known as the Royal and Ancient Golf Club of St Andrews. The game became popular in England only in the latter half of the 19th century, although the Blackheath Club was founded in the early 1800s. In 1897 the Royal and Ancient Rules were universally adopted by common consent.

Balls were originally made from soft leather stuffed with feathers, gutta-percha balls being introduced about 1848; the modern rubber-covered balls date back only to 1902.

The accepted uniform for playing golf was a red coat; whether this was purely fashion, or a safety precaution making oneself more conspicuous to other players, is not certain.

Golf

J.E. Laidlay
'putting'

John Ball Junr. Full
drive with the iron

Peter Paxton in
position for 'putting'

110

5. *Using the Beasts*

Bear Baiting with dogs was a favourite sport of the Romans and bears were imported from Britain and elsewhere for this purpose. Baiting of various animals by dogs was regular entertainment in Britain in the Middle Ages. Bulls, bears, badgers, and asses, were all used. It was a considerable gambling sport and bets were taken on how long a particular dog would last or which one would be killed first and, in some forms, the owner of the dog which jumped the highest, was the winner. It was also known for the contest to consist of man against bear, instead of dog against bear; in this event the bear was often blinded to even up the chances.

The man against beast sport has been practised since early history. In the Babylon Room of the British Museum there is a cylinder-seal showing the Assyrian heroes, Gilgamish and Eaban, wrestling with a lion and a bull.

Rome, of course, had the man against beast sport in the arenas and it was evidently a sport in Norman times, bear baiting by a man armed with a spear being depicted in the Bayeux tapestry.

Animal Baiting continued in popularity through the Tudor period, and during the reign of Henry VIII an amphitheatre to accommodate the sport was built at Bankside, Southwark. Here, at this humble imitation of a Roman amphitheatre, for the price of one halfpenny admission, one could have the pleasure of watching mastiff dogs pitched against bears.

In Elizabeth I's time a second amphitheatre was built at the Paris Gardens, and in 1582 the scaffolding supporting the spectators gave way and many were killed — perhaps the animals turned round and laughed at the poetic justice!

On the site of this bear garden the Globe Theatre was built; public interest turning to drama, but not to the exclusion of animal baiting. Sir Walter Raleigh coupled the London Bear Garden with Westminster Abbey as one of the great national sights.

The Bankside area quickly grew into one of entertainment and amusement; not only were bear gardens and the Globe Theatre situated in this, the manor of the Paris Garden, but also the Hope, the Rose, and the Swan theatres — the latter fell into

Spearing a boar, 9th century

disuse as a theatre in the time of James I and was used only for Prize Fighting.

Special strains of bears and bulls were bred for baiting, and names of some of the more famous of the bears have come down to us: Harry Hunks, Tom of Lincoln, and Blind Robin, each of which had many gory victories. The bears were, curiously enough, held in considerable esteem by their owners and keepers. One bear, called Old Nell of Middlewich, used to be taken into the local ale house for refreshment after a baiting session.

James I's Master of the Royal Bear Garden was one Edward Alleyn. It was this gentleman who founded alms houses and the Alleyn College of Dulwich, part of which was to become the Dulwich College. Alleyn sold his patent for the bear garden to his father-in-law for £580, possibly wanting to get out of the business in consequence of James I's ban on Sunday animal baiting in order to encourage the physical activities of dancing, leaping, vaulting and archery.

A monkey on horseback was usually the first item at the Bankside baiting gardens, with dogs let into the ring to frighten the horse.

Typical of the early 18th century was an advertisement of 1709 announcing a show at the New Bear Garden at Hockley-in-the-Hole — a part of Clerkenwell:

At the request of several persons of quality, on Monday the 11th of this instant of June, is one of the largest and most mischievous bears that ever was seen in England, to be baited to death, with other variety of Bull-baiting and Bear-baiting as also a wild bull to be turned loose in the game place, with fireworks all over him.

What a horrible place this must have been is even more typified in another advertisement, this time of 1730:

A mad bull to be dress'd up with fireworks over him and turned loose amongst the men in the game place. Likewise a dog to be dress'd up with fireworks over him, and turned loose with the bull amongst the men in the ground. Also a bear to be turned loose at the same time; and a cat to be tied to the bull's tail.

Surely greater mayhem is hard to imagine!

The practice of tying fireworks to animals probably had its roots in the Feast of Ceres in Rome at the time of Augustus, when foxes were turned loose in the arena with firebrands tied to their tails. This ritual was continued when the official Games of Ceres were established to the end of the 3rd century BC.

112

Horse baited with dogs

Unearthing a fox

Of Horse Baiting, the diarist, Evelyn, described how disgusted he was by the sight of the baiting of one particularly gallant horse upon which the dogs could not fasten until it had been run through by the attendants. The excuse offered for such treatment was that the horse had killed a child, but this was strongly doubted by Evelyn.

Badger Baiting is another disgusting and distasteful sport which must be included in this chapter of cruelty. It was a tavern-based baiting sport and in this one the poor animal was placed in a barrel or a drain pipe and the dogs were sent in one after the other. One of the more distasteful descriptions of the *mode d'emploi* of Badger Baiting is to be found in *The Encyclopedia of Sport* (1898), edited by The Earl of Suffolk and Berkshire, Hedley Peck and F.G. Aflalo:

They dig a place in the earth about a yard long so that one end is four feet deep. At this end a strong stake is driven down. Then the badger's tail is split, a chain put through it and fastened to the stake with such ability that the badger can come up to the other end of the place. The dogs are brought and set upon the poor animal who sometimes destroys several before it is killed.

An attempt to ban animal baiting in Britain was made in Parliament in 1802 but this was defeated by 13 votes. Another unsuccessful attempt was made in 1809 and, this time, defeated

113

Swine hunting, 9th century

by 73 votes to 28. On this occasion the sport of baiting was strongly upheld by several prominent gentlemen of the period, one declaring it, 'a manly exercise' and 'the prime cause of the growth of our population and a most necessary foundation of our military spirit'.

Animal baiting was made illegal in 1835 and, unlike cockfighting, it did not continue under cover to any great extent, although it is believed that the last bull baiting took place as late as 1853 at West Derby, Liverpool.

The Greeks of the plain of Thessaly were great horsemen and rich in herds of cattle. They developed a form of Bullfighting on horseback which was first exhibited in Rome in the 1st century BC. The method used by these Thessalian horsemen, according to Pliny, was to gallop alongside the bull and to break its neck by seizing it by the horns.

Dio described bullfighting on foot with swords and lances and it is believed this form was developed in Rome at a later date.

The sport we know today is certainly a hangover of the atrocious Roman amphitheatre sports. The Moors probably brought it to Spain, where it is the national sport. From Spain it spread with varying degrees of success, to France, back to Italy and to the Spanish influenced parts of South America. In Spain, originally, it was considered a sport for aristocrats only, the first professional bullfighter to appear being Francisco Romero of Ronda, who lived in the late 17th and early 18th centuries.

Cockfighting scenes were often represented on Athenian vases and George Jennison in his *Animals for Show and Pleasure in Ancient Rome,* says that fighting cocks in Greece were fed on leeks and onions. Pierce Egan, the 18th century sporting writer, also referred to Cockfighting as of Greek origin.

It has been said that the Romans used quail for fighting, and it is believed that these birds were used for combat in comparitively recent times in Russia.

Apart from quail, Dio in his *Epitome* mentions that the

Ladies hunting, 14th century

fighting of cranes was a Roman recreation, but it has been suggested that these exhibitions may have been mating dances!

Cockfighting was probably introduced into Britain by the Romans, but it is strange that the earliest reference we have to it in this country is by William FitzStephen who was writing in the reign of Henry II. FitzStephen who died in 1191, describes it as a countryman's sport and one for schoolboys, although he does refer to it, by way of an introduction, as a London pastime. At that time there seems to have been a considerable trade involving the importation of fighting cocks from the mainland of Europe.

To divert to inn signs for a moment, the Cock and House, or Cock House, implied a tavern at which cockfighting was staged, and the Cock and Bell sign is probably a hangover of a Shrove Tuesday custom; in this the person whose cock was victorious in the most fights won a prize of a small silver bell to be suspended from the hat, which had to be worn on three successive Sundays. The sport seems to have had considerable connection with Shrovetide; schoolchildren would take cocks to school to fight at this time, the carcasses being the 'perks' of the masters.

Cockfighting was banned in the reign of Edward III as were most other sports, to encourage the practice of archery. It was revived in the reign of Henry VIII, who had the Royal Cockpit built at Tufton Street, Westminster, and this remained in use until the early 1800s, when it was the headquarters of the sport in London. This pit is commemorated by the Cockpit Stairs which lead from Queen Anne's Gate into St James' Park.

Cockfighting had a wide appeal in London, and in addition to the one in Whitehall, there were cockpits at Drury Lane (where the theatre there was often referred to as the Cockpit Theatre), Gray's Inn Lane, Horseferry Road, Jewin Street, and Shoe Lane.

115

Bear Garden in
Southwark, 1648

Cockfighting attracted racing men, and one cockpit at which
these noble gentlemen were frequently in attendance was at
Newmarket on the site of the present Town Hall. Even minor
race meetings were often accompanied by cockfighting; in
1797, at the races on the Tunbridge Wells Town Course, there
was a Main of Cocks by the gentlemen of West Kent against the
gentlemen of East Kent. But we must not think that it was only
in the bawdy atmosphere of race meetings that the bloodthirsty
sport took place; it was also a favourite churchyard pastime.

The cockpit was usually a sanded ring 18-20ft diameter,
enclosed by a wall of about 2ft high. The fights between the
birds were of three types: Common Main, made up of 6 or 8
separate fights; Battle Royal, with 8 cocks in the ring at the
same time; and Welsh Main. In *Sports and Pastimes of the
People of England*, Strutt writes: 'the Welsh Main is the abuse
of modern times'. In this form of combat, a number of pairs of
cocks, usually 8 or 16, fought until half the number were killed.
The winners were pitted again until another half were slain,
and so on, until the fight of the last pair was finished.

The prizes for cockfighting were not large considering the
expense that went into breeding and preparing the cocks, even
in those days when cash had so much more value. At a Main
fought at the Morpeth Pit on 20 February 1844, the winner was
awarded a heifer valued at £15, the second prize being £5 in
cash. The winner of the two battles was given thirty shillings
and the winner of one battle ten shillings.

The names of the cocks were colourful. For instance, a Mr
Duncomb Shafto, active until 1839 and described as a 'mighty
cocker', owned such birds as Wilks, Liberty, I have to withstand
thee, I will show you how, Come in the morning, North
Country lad, and Little thought of.

116

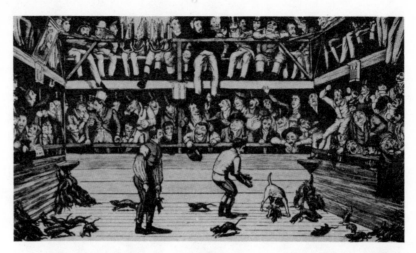

Public feeling against cockfighting was building up and in
April 1841 a certain Jonathan Briggs was found guilty of
keeping and using a garden at Glenthan, near Lincoln, for the
purpose of Cockfighting. Information had been laid by an
agent of the National Society for the Prevention of Cruelty to
Animals, and Briggs was fined £5 3s with costs.

Although cockfighting was made illegal by Act of
Parliament in 1849, what was probably the last public pit in
England was not closed until 1874, when a police raid put an
end to its activities. This was the Galloway Gate Pit, connected
with the Bay Horse Inn, Newcastle-on-Tyne. However, the
sport continued under cover and the authorities closed many an
eye, particularly in such counties as Staffordshire and
Westmorland, where the Fighting Cocks is a favourite inn sign.
We read in *The Dalesman*, The Yorkshire magazine, that there
are traces of cockpits around the Sutton-in-Craven district,
'grassy mounds, all in secluded places and quite definitely
excavated'.

King Solomon said of the greyhound, 'it goes well and is
comely in going'. Still in ancient history, Arrian describes
something like the sport of Coursing in his *Cynegetious* in the
2nd century AD. There is a certain mystique connected with the
greyhound, a breed thought to have been introduced into
England by the Celts. In 1016, there was a statute in which King
Canute forbade anyone under the rank of gentleman to own a
greyhound; and in Stuart times there were laws forbidding
anyone with less than a certain value of property from owning
this breed of hound, these laws still being in force in the 18th
century.

The first set of coursing rules was drawn up in Tudor times
by the Duke of Norfolk. The title covering these rules was the

Dog and Monkey
Fight

*Laws of the Leash or Coursing, as they were commanded,
allowed, and subscribed by Thomas, late Duke of Norfolk, in
the reign of Queen Elizabeth.* These rules were in force until the
latter part of the 18th century, when they underwent something
of a revolution.

A form of the sport was the 17th century activity called
Paddock Coursing. This used a strip of grassland about a mile
long and a quarter of a mile wide, enclosed by fences. At one
end of the strip cages were built for dogs and for the quarry, a
deer or a stag. Posts were driven into the ground at 160yds,
¼mile, and ½mile intervals. Between the ½mile marker and the
end of the strip a ditch was dug. The stag was released, so too
was a *teaser* dog to keep the unfortunate beast moving, and
when the 160yds post was reached the hounds were released.
The winner was the hound that caught the stag or was nearest
to the ditch when, or rather if, the quarry was lucky enough to
cross to safety.

The Scottish sport of Deer Stalking is one involving
considerable skill, as the animal has most sensitive hearing and
can also detect the smell of a human at quite a long range.
There are two modes of Deer Stalking: quiet Stalking, in which
the stalker creeps up silently on his quarry; and Stalking in
Double Quick Time or Driving Deer, in which the quarry is
driven towards the guns.

Early Wildfowlers made use of the crossbow, net and line,
and a horse, cow or ox, behind which the stalker could hide. We
read that Henry VIII had his own stalking horse. Sometimes
instead of a live hide, a stuffed canvas horse would be used.

In 1860 a Colonel Russell, leading a party of 32 punt guns on
the river Blackwater, shot and picked up the astounding bag of

118

704 wild geese. Later, another 250 or so were found dead along the banks by local people. A celebration breakfast was taken at the Green Man, Bradwell-Juxton-Mare — justifiably so, as the record still stands.

Dog Fighting was still permitted by law after 1849, when Cockfighting was declared illegal, but it was a sport that never caught the public's imagination to any great extent.

Animal fighting has taken many forms over the years and in many parts of the world. One of the more unusual forms of animal combat is the Mongoose and Snake fight performed in India, the former animal being noted for its ability to fight and kill snakes.

Seneca mentions a fight between a bear and a bull tied together in the Roman arena, and we read of elephant duels from Pliny.

There seems no end to the ingenuity of man when he applies his mind to pitting one animal against another. The sport in India of mongoose against snake could possibly be justified, as such combat is natural in that country, but the event that was held on 26 July 1825, at the Green Dragon, Warwick, seems completely indefensible. This was a fight between a lion and a number of dogs. The suffering is said to have been great but it is slightly refreshing to learn that it met with almost universal condemnation in the press of the day.

A less barbarous type of animal combat is Camel Fighting, which is said to have been practised by the Greeks for centuries before the Christian era. In modern times it has become almost entirely restricted to Asian Turkey.

The camels used for fighting are usually cross-bred between the one-humped Arabian (dromedary) and the two-humped Bactrian varieties. The breeding is a very specialised business, almost akin to that of the breeding of race horses.

It seems more humane than other forms of animal fighting, and to prevent the camels from biting each other, they have their mouths bound with twine. The winner is the animal to put his adversary on the ground.

The extremely cruel sport, referred to in 1665 as the 'Royal Diversion of Duck Hunting', is another example of man's lack of feeling for the sufferings of animals. It was played on the duck ponds at semi-rural inns around London.

The largest of the London duck ponds was that kept by a Mr Ball, an innkeeper in what is now the Ball's Pond Road. Here were several acres of water where one could fish for carp, engage in duck hunting or in shooting.

Probably the last of London's duck ponds was the one in

Bruton Street, Mayfair, where there is still a Ducking Pond Mews to commemorate the site.

A duck with clipped wings, and often tied by the leg was released on the pond. The inn customers' dogs were *sicked on* (a term of the day) to catch it. If the dog caught the duck, the owner could keep the carcass but if the duck survived for a certain length of time the dog's owner had to pay a fee. Of course, the bookmakers did a roaring trade.

The inn sign of the Dog and Duck are now reminders of this sport.

Another nasty duck pond activity was the owl and duck fight. For this an owl was tied on the back of a duck and both birds released. The owl pecked away at the duck's head and the duck tried to get rid of the owl by diving into the water. The contest went on until either the duck died from the owl's attack or the owl was drowned.

> We'll banish all sorrow
> And sing till to-morrow
> And angle and angle again.
>
> Izaak Walton.

Swift did not share Walton's delight; his definition of angling was, 'a stick and a string, a worm at one end and a fool at the other'. There are numerous examples of ancient Egyptian fishhooks which are like those of modern designs and it would seem reasonable to suppose that this method of catching fish with a hook has been known for a very long time.

Although in modern times, the term *angling* is used to indicate the capture of fish by rod, line and hook, the original Anglo Saxon expression *angel* simply meant the use of a hook.

There is an unlikely reference to angling in the 15th century book by Dame Juliana Berners, Prioress of Sopwell, near St Albans. This book, entitled *The Boke of St Albans* contains a treatise on *Fysshynge With An Angle*. There is a description of the tackle used in that time: a 9ft long willow or hazel branch was hollowed out with red hot irons; to the top of this was fitted a 3ft length of hazel and then 4-5ft of whippy blackthorn, crab or juniper wood. The line, tied to the tip of the rod, was made from six times plaited hairs from the tail of a white horse; the line was dyed with a vegetable colour, the shade depending on the condition of the water and the season — green when the water was clear, yellow in autumn and brown in winter. Floats were made of cork and hooks from needles.

According to Dame Juliana, another method of catching fish was to use a goose, to the leg of which was tied a live frog. To the

Fishing at Olney
Bridge,
Buckinghamshire

other leg was tied a long line. The goose was then set free on the water. A fish would take the frog. The goose would bob a little, at which sign the fisherman would haul in his goose.

It was not until the 19th century that sophisticated tackle became commercially available and until then anglers had to prepare their own. Fishing was considered something of a peasant pastime but at the time of the industrial revolution it began to rival football and cricket in the built-up areas, with workers seeking a sample of country.

We must look to Homer for some of the first references to Sea Angling. To quote the Odyssey (XII 251):

Even as where a fisher on some headland lets down with a long rod his baits for a snare to the little fishes below, casting into the deep the horn of an ox of the homestead, and as he catches each flings it writhing ashore, so writhing were they (the companions of Odyssus) borne upward to the cliff.

The reference to 'the horn of an ox of the homestead' has brought forth many theories over the years. Some have suggested that the horn might be a guard around the line where it meets the hook or even the hook itself, but it is now almost universally accepted that this was a sliver of horn acting as a spinner to attract the fish.

By definition, Hawking and Falconry is the art of taking game by means of trained hunting birds.

121

Saxon Hawking, 9th
century

Sir S. Layard, writing in the 19th century on finds in the
ruins of Khorsabad, mentions the discovery of a figure of 'a
falconer bearing a hawk upon his wrist'. This would suggest
that falconry existed about 1200 BC. It is also thought that
falconry was practised in China about 2000 BC and in Japan
about 600 BC. It was mentioned by Aristotle, Pliny and Martial,
but the first reference we have to the sport in England comes in
748 AD in a letter from King Ethelbert to St Boniface,
Archbishop of Mayence, the king requesting two falcons. It was
during this century that Hawking became the pastime of the
nobility and the rich. So prized were these birds that the offence
of stealing the hawk's eggs was punishable by imprisonment
for a year and a day; a penalty that persisted for centuries. In her
compassion, Elizabeth I reduced this sentence to one of three
months.

In broad terms, the difference between the two classes of the
sport are these: Falconry involves the birds with long wings, the
Hawks being shorter-winged species.

Several traditional terms connected with the sport have come
down to us. An Eyas is a hawk which has been reared by hand; a
Ramage Hawk is one captured when young; and a Haggard
Hawk, logically, is one captured when fully grown.

A Stanniel is a kestrel with the characteristics of a noble
falcon. The Gerfalcons and Little Hobbies also had these
characteristics. One way by which a noble falcon was identified
was by the fact that it had a brown eye; whereas the ignoble
falcon had a yellow or white eye.

The Muskyte or Musket was the term adopted for firearms, as
originally the name given to the bird indicated that it had to be
thrown towards the quarry. A bird gave its name to another
firearm — the Falconet.

Some everyday words have come down to us from the sport;
the term *bousing,* meaning that a hawk is drinking deeply, gave
rise to our slang expression *boozing,* and, of course, *hoodwink*
has its roots in the sport.

Falconry was still considered a rich man's sport in the 17th

Hawking

122

The Falkoner *(sic)*

century. For instance, the Duke of Bedford's Chief Falconer received an income of £120 per annum, whereas his huntsmen were paid only £16.

As the use of firearms increased in the 18th century, hawking spread more and more to the humbler classes, while the rich began to favour their new toys.

From the earliest times Hunting has been necessary for survival. Until the idea of farming and breeding occurred, to man his only means of staying alive was to take his sling or his bow and arrows, and then go out to 'shop' for his meal. Not only did man kill for food; wild animals were a threat to human life itself, and hunting parties had to be formed to eliminate wild animals that raided the settlements.

Fox Hunting

Lion Hunting from chariots was a favourite sport of Assyrian kings and this served the double purpose of killing off dangerous beasts and providing an exciting sport. In the British Museum there is a bas-relief depicting such a hunt, which was taken from the palace of Assur-Nasir-Pal, king of Assyria (c. 885-860 BC) at Calash (Nimrud). The hunters in the chariot are using bows and arrows.

In Britain it is thought to have been the Saxons who began to consider the hunting of animals as a sport. Their quarries were the wolf, the bear and the wild boar.

By the time the Normans had conquered the land the wilder animals were fast becoming extinct and it was the hart, the stag, the hind, the roebuck, and the mertin cat that took the fancy of the sportsman.

The fox was considered an inferior animal to chase and it was not until the 14th century that we have the first mention of Fox Hunting, when Richard II granted a charter to the Abbot of Peterborough to hunt the animal.

During the reigns of the Tudors all kinds of hunting took on great popularity and these excursions became occasions of great formality. But it was not the participant sport it became later; it was more a spectacle allied to coursing. Grandstands and hunting lodges were built along the chase and in these the nobility in their finery would take up their positions to watch the huntsman ride down the released animals. When Elizabeth I rode to the Enfield Chase in 1557 she was accompanied by twelve ladies in white satin and a company of yeoman with gilded bows. It is reported that Elizabeth herself made a kill that day. Blood lust had taken over from necessity hunting, and

124

Stag Hunting, 1671

Otter Hunting, 1611

killing for food had become the province of the poacher.

The rise of fox hunting may partly have been a result of the Civil War. During that period a great many deer were killed in a wanton way with no regard to replacing their number. People therefore turned to the hare and the fox as animals to hunt for sport. This shortage of game may well have been the cause of a law of 1671 which forbade a freeholder of less than £100 and a leaseholder of less than £150 to shoot game, even on his own land — a foolish law, as it made criminals out of many law-abiding citizens and poachers out of anyone who hunted for food.

Wild Duck Shooting

The real home of fox hunting in the 18th century was the North, and it was at Caldbeck, Cumberland, in 1779 that the most famous huntsman of all was born. During the early years of the 19th century, John Peel, then an innkeeper, owned the Caldbeck hounds.

That other great sportsman, Squire George Osbaldeston (known as 'the squire of all England'), 1786-1866, famous marksman, cricketer, boxer, jockey, oarsman, coach driver, gambler and billiard player, was Master of Foxhounds in Northamptonshire in the early years of the 19th century. Melton Mowbray was a great hunting area for Osbaldeston. Here, according to his friend, 'Nimrod', writing in 1837, were the Old Club and the New Club. He writes, 'the old Club was most respectable with only four bedrooms'. The New Club was accommodated in Lord Alvanley's house opposite the George Hotel.

Towards the end of the 18th century there was developed a sport known as the Fox Match. This involved two couples of hounds competing against each other to take the fox first. The Earl of Effingham was a supporter of this form of sport and many of these Fox Matches took place around the areas of Wetherby and Thornville, in Yorkshire.

Pig Sticking or Hog Sticking is the sport of impaling wild boars by a spear from horseback. In India, spearing was considered by the British the only sportsmanlike way of killing a boar. It was a seasonal sport lasting from February to July, a period set by those who conceived the sport in the latter part of the 18th century. It began with the riding down and spearing of small bears, and when these creatures became scarce the sportsmen turned their attention to the boar and liked what they found. The boar was called by Colonel Heber Percy, in the *Badminton Library* volume on Big Game, 'the pluckiest of all beasts' and he records cases of boars chasing men and even

Baiting a Lion

killing tigers; it was this courage that caused Pig Sticking to be the premier sport in India in the late 19th century.

Rat Killing gained popularity after the banning of animal baiting and cockfighting, particularly in rural areas. The idea was for either individuals or teams to compete against each other. Ferrets and dogs were used to chase the rats from holes, when they were either clubbed to death or caught by dogs. Another method was to catch the rats in traps and then release them for the dogs to course.

In the early part of the 20th century live rats were commanding the price of several shillings each for sporting purposes.

During the 18th century a form of competition amongst sailors was for groups of men to go down to the holds and wager how many rats a man could kill with his teeth, his hands being tied behind his back.

One of the most distasteful of animal sports to be found anywhere in the 18th century was the practice of Goose Pulling. The idea was to hang a goose by its legs from a pole or a tree branch. The contestants then galloped past in turn and

127

attempted to grab at the creature's neck. The one who succeeded in pulling off the goose's head was the winner. One can detect a certain Quintain influence in this sport although it did not have the element of risk of being hit back.

In the tradition of Shying At Cocks, which the Europeans evolved with religious signifigance, the American settlers enjoyed the sport of Shooting At Tethered Bears and Turkeys. There is no evidence in this case that it was connected with any ritual or season of the year.

In the strict sense of the Spanish word, Rodeo means *ride* — and implies the rounding up of cattle in order to have them branded. Over the years in America it has come to mean any kind of sporting event in which horsemanship and usually Steer Roping and Wrestling are the predominant features.

In Chile the Gauchos give exhibitions of a more genuine type of Rodeo with less stunting. Items include demonstrations of rounding up and cutting out of cattle.

Another South American Rodeo competition is one in which the object is to bump young bulls against wattle shields by riding them into the fence.

The Topeadura is played all over rural Chile and not only at Rodeos. In this event two teams of riders and their horses, of any equal number, line up on either side of a bar — a log supported about 3ft off the ground — with the object of pushing the opposing team away from the bar.

So ends this chapter on the use and often painful and sorrowful abuse of living creatures for pleasure and sport.

6. Games for Fun

Games, like other recreational pastimes, probably had their origins in man's two great needs: to survive, and for a faith and devotion in a power superior to the species. Training and exercise for hunting and labour, teaching and ritualistic expression of faith and the accompanying codes of morality, were the motives for games.

In this chapter, even if some of the games seem ludicrous, we can see the teaching and exercise motives, albeit hidden under layers of environmental change.

The old West of England game of Tinkeler's Shop (or Tinker's Shop) was in a group of pastimes which had the quickening of reactions as an object rather than victory. William Hone, writing in 1826, mentions Tinkeler's Shop as being played in his time, but it seems impossible to discover when it was discontinued.

The setting for this remarkable game was usually the village tavern or sometimes outside on the green. All who wanted to take part would kneel down in a circle round a large iron pot filled with a mixture of soot and water. Beside this pot stood the Master of the Shop. Everyone was provided with a short stick and, in addition, the Master held a mop. The Master allocated everyone a name such as Old Vulcan, Save All, Tear-Em, All My Men, Mend-All, and so on. He then shouted out, 'One and all', upon which the game began with everyone knocking on the ground with their sticks. Suddenly the Master again called out and this time named one or more of the players, such as 'Old Vulcan and Mend-All'. Everyone except those so named had to stop knocking. If anyone made a mistake the penalty was a swipe round the face with a mop after it had been dipped in the pot, the winner being the last player with a clean face.

Another West Country game which, according to William Hone, was still being played at the beginning of the 19th century was the Corn Market, a game with a family resemblance to Tinkeler's Shop. To start, a Market Master was appointed together with an assistant, given the name of Spy the Market, and a strange character, Old Penglaze. The latter was foolishly dressed, his face blackened, carrying a staff in his hand and riding a hobby-horse. All the other players sat in a circle

Round Tag

129

and were given price tags to wear round their necks: '2 pence', '3 pence', '4 pence' and so on.

The Master called, 'Spy the Market', to which his assistant replied, 'Aye Sirrah'. The Master then asked the price of a commodity, such as barley, and his assistant shouted out any price he chose, for example '2 pence'. The price was repeated and the player who had been given that price had to call 'Aye Sirrah'. If anyone missed his cue or if someone else called out wrongly, the Master would go up to the offender and pick up one of his feet, calling out, 'Here is my seal. Where is Old Penglaze's seal?' Old Penglaze then came into the circle mounted on his hobby-horse, calling out, 'Here I come, neither riding nor on foot. What work is there for me to do?' The master held up the culprit's foot saying, 'Here Penglaze, there is a shoeing match for you'. Replied Penglaze, 'I think it's a fine colt indeed', pulling off the shoe from the victim and uttering this strange incantation, 'My reward is a full gallon of moonlight, besides all other customs for shoeing in this market', and giving two sharp raps on the shoeless foot with his staff. The game continued, ending in a dance.

A more recent equivalent to these forfeit games may be found in a drinking game simply known as Fingers. In this, all the players are allocated a sign, such as two fingers crossed or three fingers outstretched, or other signs of this kind. A chairman is appointed who makes a sign, which has to be identified immediately by the person who has been given that sign. The game goes on until one of the players makes a mistake, whereupon everyone shouts 'drink', and the loser has to drink whatever is in his glass. Two mistakes means that the next round of drinks has to be paid for by the loser.

In the old tavern game of Hopping the Twig the contestant held a twig in front of him with both hands and attempted to jump over it, drawing the twig behind him and land with his feet in a position on the ground behind the place from which he had started, and without breaking the twig. The positions were marked, and the winner of the contest was the person who landed at the rearmost mark.

Kicking the Beam is a tavern game the author remembers seeing as a boy at the White Hart — known locally as the Bo-Peep — near Chelsfield in Kent. On Sunday mornings it was the practice of the regular customers to challenge one another to a kicking match, the target being a beam in the ceiling of the pub just about 6ft above the floor.

Perhaps the funniest game of all in the tavern class was Drawing the Dun from the Mire, although it could not have been all that amusing to play. In fact, to say it was uncomfortable is a gross understatement. But in those pre-Tudor days, when it was played in rural areas, life was rugged indeed.

To play Drawing the Dun from the Mire, all that was needed was a tree-trunk and an unlimited number of players. The large log was intended to represent the 'dun' or cart horse, and was placed on some soft ground. The game started with two players coming forward to lift the log, at the same time chanting, 'the dun is in the mire' over and over again. Of course they could not get it off the ground and were joined by others until successful. Then the fun began. Earlier, while drinking, groups of the players had arranged signals such as winks and nods, and these groups, using the signals, would attempt to drop the log on the toes of the others. Everyone had the same thing in mind and the operation came down to one of timing.

A tavern game, but not confined to that environment, is Hands, Up Jenkins, or Tippet (sometimes known as Tippit). It is a popular game in the South West of England and is also played in northern France as a traditional Whitsuntide game, where it is called Ferret. At least three players are required in each of the two teams who sit facing each other across a long table. One team passes a coin along under the table, trying not to disclose who actually has the coin. The captain of the opposing team may shout at any time, 'Up Jenkins' or 'Smash', when all the members of the other team hit their hands down hard on the table. The opposing captain will then shout, 'Crawl', which means that the players must *walk* their hands along the table while trying to conceal which player has the coin. The game ends with members of the opposing team guessing which hand holds the coin. The game is also known as Cod'em or Kid'em.

One may think of the Up Jenkins group of games as being adult versions of the old party games of Hunt the Thimble and Hunt the Slipper and it must remain a matter of speculation as to which came first.

It is astounding what people will do or attempt, to show their skills or prove physical abilities. There have been and are some quite ridiculous sports and games, some of which have come to be accepted as normal.

Climbing the Greasy Pole is an event that has survived the passage of time and is still an attraction at village fetes. The traditional prize at the old revels was a large piece of bacon tied to the top of the pole, this going to the first person who could climb the pole and cut down the prize.

Allied to this, but seeming to have more to do with quarter-staff fighting, is the Pillow Fight, with a pole supported in a horizontal position, the contestants sitting astride the pole and trying to knock one another to the ground or, in some cases, into water below. A junior derivative is called Branch Boy. In this game two boys hang by their hands from a branch of a tree and attempt to push each other off.

Grinning through the Horsecollar is a particularly amusing event and typical of the more gentle attractions at country revels in the 18th century, but one which seems to have died, through the scarcity of horsecollars. On the other hand, we still have Ugly Face Contests (without the horsecollar) surviving to some extent. Grinning, sometimes called *gerning*, in the context of this activity means the pulling of an ugly face, the winner being the person judged to have caused the most laughs. To grin, according to *Chambers' Twentieth-Century English Dictionary*, is 'to set the teeth together and withdraw the lips; to smile with some accompanying distortion of the features, expression of derision, stupid admiration'. The winner was traditionally awarded a hat invariably described as a 'good hat'.

Like Grinning through the Horsecollar, the Whistling Match was one of the more amusing and harmless of the activities that went on at taverns and country fairs, and another that unfortunately seems to have been forgotten over the years. The contestants lined up and started to whistle a merry tune. The village clown or comic then danced round in front of them pulling faces in an attempt to stop them whistling. The game went on until there was only one non-stop whistler. There is something of a survival of this game in the childish joke of sucking a lemon or an orange in front of a wind player in a brass band at the seaside or in the park.

At fairs and revels of old, there was an event rudely called Old Women Drinking Hot Tea, which could perhaps be considered the female equivalent of the male marathon beer-drinking contests.

Other country fair events, particularly in the 18th century, included Hasty Pudding Eating, with the winner being the contestant who could consume the greatest number of plum puddings, and Smoking Races with prizes awarded for the fastest pipeful smoked and for the one lasting the longest. A hat was the traditional prize in the Smoking Races.

Catching a soaped pig used to be a popular attraction at country fairs for many years, certainly from the 18th century. With its tail cut short so that it could not be grasped, the pig was let loose and the first person to catch it could then take it away.

A variation on the animal-catching theme used to take place at Kidlington, Oxfordshire, on the Monday after Whit Week. Girls had their thumbs tied behind their backs and the object of the exercise was to run after and catch a lamb with the teeth. The winner was then proclaimed the Lady of the Lamb for the following year and in her honour there was a feast.

Men Ploughing for Breeches was a fair and revel activity that served as a good opportunity for the competitors to show off their skill in ploughing a straight furrow and so enhance their chances of continued employment. We still have ploughing matches with tractors and occasionally with horses, but where have all the breeches gone?

Although Egg Shackling is perhaps more a custom than a game it has the competition element needed for inclusion in this chapter. It is still observed at Shrovetide at several places including Stoke St Gregory, Taunton and Shepton Beauchamp near Sedgmoor. The children write their names on eggs and take them to school on Shrove Tuesday. Here all the eggs are placed in a sieve and shaken well until only one remains unbroken, and the child with his or her name on this egg receives a prize. The origin of this custom is obscure, but undoubtedly it is related to other Shrovetide activities of using up food before Lent. Mrs Harper, the headteacher of the school at Stoke St Gregory, tells me that the school logbook records the event in 1864, and mentions it then as an old custom.

At Stockton-on-Tees the children had their own particular egg game. Firstly, the hard-boiled eggs were rolled down a lane from The Green, as in the traditional Pace Egg custom. They were then subjected to *Jarping* or *Jauping*. The challenge was 'I'll jaup you', when the eggs were battered together end-on, the winner being the owner of the egg that lasted the longest. Stockton Egg Jarping was not exclusively a children's game. A public house called The Grey Horse, which stood in Stockton High Street until it was recently demolished, used to be the scene of a contest in which only tapping and no rolling was involved.

During the Middle Ages the games played by children were Blindman's Buff, Penny Prick (Prykke), Piggy in the Ring, Snap Dragon, and Hand In Hand Out. Unfortunately the methods of play of the last three have been lost in the course of time, but it is thought that the old game of Snap Dragon may have been something like the game we know by the same name in this and the last century. This was played by soaking a bowlful of raisins in brandy and setting them alight, the object then being for the players to grab as many raisins as possible through the flames.

133

Later, in Tudor times, apart from Blindman's Buff, Hot Cockles, and chasing games, there developed the seeking breed of games which included Hunt the Slipper, Hunt the Ring and Hunt the Thimble.

An interesting branch of children's games is that requiring skills in keeping something in motion. Whip Tops and Peg Tops are the obvious examples of this family, but we must also remember Keeping Feathers in the Air, Bouncing a Ball on a Stick, and Spinning Coins. The latter is certainly related to a party game called Trencher. In this a bread board is spun, someone's name is called, and he has to grasp the board before it topples over.

Children have been happy with their own improvised games, and even in these days of sophistication we can see what classics some of the old games have become. Such an example is O'Grady Says which is in direct line of descent from the ancient Greek game of Basilinda. The leader stands in front of the others calling out, 'O'Grady says, do *this*', and everyone has to do it. On the other hand, if the leader calls, 'O'Grady says do *that*', the order must not be obeyed. Throughout the ages there have been variations on the theme, and this can be recognised in such games as Follow my Leader.

Many games played in the 20th century can be traced to Roman and pre-Roman times. Piling was a game played by children of Rome in which nuts were used. The object was for each player to add a nut alternatively until the pile fell down — the last player being the loser. An element of this game can be found in a current tavern activity using matchsticks instead of nuts, and playing for drinks.

Directly opposed to Piling is the name known under the several names of Spillikins, Spelicans, Juggling Straws, Jerk Straws or Jack Straws (Probably after Wat Tyler's lieutenant in the Peasant's Revolt of 1381). In this game a number of pointed sticks are thrown down haphazardly and the object is to pick up as many as possible separately and without disturbing the remainder. Some very charming Victorian examples of this game with carved ivory sticks have survived.

> The spring clad all in gladness
> Doth laugh at winter's sadness,
> And to the bag-pipe's sound
> The nymphs tread out the ground.
>
> Fie then! Why sit we musing.
> Youth's sweet delight refusing?
> Say, dainty nymphs and speak,
> Shall we play at Barley-Break?   Anonymous (1595)

The game of Barley Break must be one of the oldest games

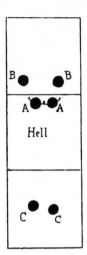

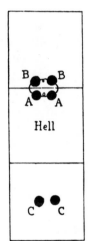

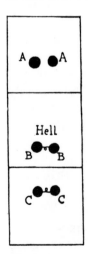

Barley Break

involving the taking of prisoners. Its mere name carries a considerable ring of antiquity and the method of play has more than a suggestion of a fertility ritual.

Allusions are made to Barley Break by Burton, Massinger, Sidney, Suckling, and Herrick, and it seems safe to assume that it was well known as a rustic game before the 16th century. Unfortunately no really reliable contemporary descriptions of the game can be found, but from what can be gleaned it is thought that whole villages used to enact the game in a field divided into three parts. The players paired up in couples (male and female), a third of their number going into each section of the field. Those allocated to the middle section — called 'Hell' (and giving its name to the game's other title, Last Couple in Hell) — ran round chasing the other couples and dragging them into 'Hell', the last couple to be caught being the winner.

Iona and Peter Opie's impression of the game is somewhat different. In their book, *Children's Games in Street and Playground*, they compounded the descriptions in Sidney's *Arcadia* (c. 1580), Nicholas Briton's *Barley-Breake, or a Warning to Wantons* (c.1607), and Suckling's *Fragmenta Aurea* (1646), and from these decided that only three couples took part — just one couple being stationed in 'Hell'. The other players then attempted to *change partners*. If intercepted they had to change placed with a player of the same sex already in 'Hell'. A series of two or three 'breaks' — attempts at changing partners — were made.

According to William Hone, writing in 1827, the game Barley Break was played in the fields of Yorkshire and Scotland at harvest time. In Scotland the game was called Barla Breikis or Barla Braks. In this version a certain stack was nominated as the goal to which the hunting couple dragged the others. The stack was called the 'dule'. It is believed that the game was still played in the early part of the 20th century in Cumberland, where it was known as Barley Brigs. Barla Braks seems to have a relationship to the Lanarkshire farm game of Stacks, mentioned in Alice Bertha Gomme's *Traditional Games of England, Scotland and Ireland* (1894). This was a seeking and chasing game in which kisses were exchanged between the boys and the girls.

The game of Prisoner's Base (Bars or Bays) — also known as French and English — was, in all probability, a derivative of Barley Break, but in this game the players are divided into two teams, the object being to take prisoners by touching as many opponents as possible. It has also been said that this version of the classic 'tag' or catching game may have originated after the battle of Agincourt and the name of French and English may

135

have been given to it at that time. Joseph Strutt mentions seeing a 'grand game' of Prisoner's Base played in 1770 in the grounds of Montague House, where the British Museum now stands, between teams of twelve men each from Cheshire and Derbyshire for a 'considerable sum of money'.

The game, as played by children in the 20th century, takes place on a marked-out ground, with the distance from the bases to the prisons being about 25yds. The bases must be large enough to contain all the players of one side standing in a line. Any number can take part, but the optimum team is one of between ten and fifteen players. The captain who loses the toss must send out a 'chivy' — a player whose task is to act as a decoy standing in the centre of the field. When he arrives at this station he calls out 'chivy' whereupon one of the opposing team sets out in pursuit in an attempt to 'tag' him. The decoy may then run either to one of the prisons or home to base where he is safe. His pursuer is in turn chased by a player of the chivy's team and so on until all the players are on the field. A player who touches or captures another must then make his way back to base and start again. Prisoners — those who are 'tagged' — are sent to the area marked as their prison and may then be released by a member of their own team who has to run from home to prison without being touched. The result usually depends on a time limit, at the end of which the winning side is the one with the largest number of prisoners. Alternatively, the game ends when all the players of one side are in prison.

Prisoner's Base is a game of considerable antiquity. Its prohibition in the vicinity of the Royal Palace when Parliament was sitting is specifically mentioned in a statute of 1332.

In the children's game of Release a chaser is picked whose object is to put as many of the other players as possible into 'prison' — a semi-circle marked on the ground. Other free members can get them out by calling 'release' or 'relievo' and pulling their team-mates out of the semi-circle. If a chaser is able to catch them while they are still holding hands, they both go to prison. When all the players are safely inside, the last prisoner becomes the chaser and the game starts again.

Goal Running is another game closely related to Prisoner's Base. As far as researches disclose, it was played only in Kent and East Sussex up to the early 1950s and was considered an important adult sport played by both men and women. There was even a Goal Running League which comprised teams from Tenterden, Whitstable, Herne Bay, Ore, Faversham and Hythe. Any number of people could take part, but usually about twenty-two made a good team. The field is best described as a triangle with a goal flag at the apex and each of the two teams' bases at the other corners. Midway between the bases and the goal there were 'point' flags. Members of the teams began running in succession from their bases, round the point flag and returning to base. At any time one of the players could make a run for goal and, if he succeeded in rounding the flag and returning to base without being touched by a member of the other team (who could run across the pitch for this purpose), he scored two points. If he were touched, two points were awarded to the other team.

Capturing games were not only played outdoors. One, which could be considered a distant cousin, was the Cushion Dance and was popular at parties in the 19th century. In this game a cushion was placed in the centre of the floor and all the players joined hands and danced round it. The idea was to pull each other on to the cushion, anyone who fell on to it being dismissed, until only one player remained. There is an obvious connection between the Cushion Dance and Musical Chairs. It is probable that the mode of play and the name were inspired by the Cushion Dance which was carried on at wakes and celebrations up to the 18th century, but this really was a dance and not a game.

The simple game of Tag, in which one child is appointed 'he' or 'it' and who touches one of them who then becomes 'he', must be one of the oldest and natural games to have survived through the ages. The origin, if ever it had such a moment, is lost in the mists of antiquity.

A particularly robust version of a 'tagging' game was played in the North of England up to the early years of the 20th century and known as Gaffers. The boy appointed as 'he' carried a whip and ran among the rest of the boys trying to catch one of them. When caught, the victim had to stand with his hands above his head and take several lashes with the whip. This game may have had its origin in the Leicester semi-game custom of the Whipping Toms, which followed a traditional annual game of hockey. The Toms were men dressed in a kind of uniform, some state this to consist of a blue smock, a few of their number carried hand bells while others had long whips, lashing out at all except their fellow Toms. Now and then a man would arm himself with a stick and parry off the lash of the whip, paying a small fine if unsuccessful. From a description of this practice in the *Year Book* by William Hone, it appears that three men were appointed as the Whipping Toms who were attended by a fourth man carrying a bell. The game was, according to Hone, to try to silence the bell man, for when he was unable to ring his bell, the Toms were powerless to use their whips. The Toms

137

were not allowed to whip above the knees and one way to gain immunity was to kneel down.

According to an exchange of correspondence between the Curator of the Leicester Museum and the author, there is some doubt that the Whipping Toms practice followed a hockey match. This assertion appears in Christina Hole's *English Sports and Pastimes* (1949), but John Throsby, in *History of Leicester* (1791), reported that the 'amusement' was confined to the ancient custom of the Whipping Toms.

As far as the origin of the Whipping Toms is concerned, John Throsby wrote it was 'originally instituted by the dwellers in the Newarke to drive away the rabble after a certain hour from the fair', but it is more popularly supposed to commemorate the expulsion of the Danes from Leicester on Hoke Day in 1002. The custom became unpopular and was eventually banned under the Leicester Improvement Act of 1846. The Whipping Toms did not die without a struggle and the following year saw a serious clash between the public and the police when the Toms tried to enforce their game.

It is curious that a parallel can be found in the villages of the remoter parts of Asia in a game in which the contestants make alternate strokes with a whip while another defends himself with a stick.

Finally, on the subject of violent games, the one which is probably the most vicious of all must not be forgotten — that of Running the Gantlet, in which the victim has to run between two rows of people each hitting out with weapons of their choice. An ancient Nordic form of punishment for criminals, it became a game in the days when pastimes were as tough as the period in which the people lived. There is no connection with the gauntlet, a protective glove; the word in this case means a line or a street. A version of Running the Gantlet was played at Stornaway, on the Isle of Lewis, as part of the children's game of Three Lives. The running in this game takes the form of rushing through a tunnel formed by every child putting one hand against a wall.

Somewhere, sometime in Tudor days blindfold games were introduced into the merry-making scene. At fairs and revels adults indulged in Jingling Matches, Bell Races, and Blindfold Wheelbarrow Races. Children also had their blindfold activities at home and in the field, including Blindman's Buff, Hot Cockles, Blowing Out the Candle, Brother I'm Bobbed, Buff With the Wand, and Blind Postman.

Jingling Matches featured at public merrymaking well into the 19th century. There were usually about ten competitors, involved, one of whom had to know the procedure of the game one of whom had bells attached to his knees and elbows. The others were blindfolded. A match lasted for about half an hour and if the jingling player could evade his pursuers for that period he was declared the winner, otherwise the prize went to the captor. Another and later jingling game which involved only two players — one blindfolded — was called Cat and Mouse, among other names, depending on the area in which it was played.

Bell Races were variations of Jingling Matches with all the competitors blindfolded and having to run in the direction of a ringing bell, usually at a distance of about 100yds. Real wheel-barrows were originally used in Blindfold Wheelbarrow Races, although more recently the barrows have been replaced by the 'pusher' holding the legs of someone walking on his hands.

Blindman's Buff or Hoodman Blind is the converse form of the Jingling Match, with only one player being blindfolded and having to catch any of the other players. Once touched, a player has to don the blindfold and take up the role of the pursuer. Often the 'blind man' has to guess the identity of the person touched as a qualification to rid himself of his blindfold. Undoubtedly this is a very old form of recreation. Hoodwinke Play is mentioned by John Hurst in 1573. The *hood* part of the game's name came from the method of 'blinding' the chaser by reversing the hood on his head. Sometimes, in days gone by, the players whipped out at the hoodman with a cloth or scarf. We are inclined to think of Blindman's Buff as a childish activity, but in past ages — and it is a very old game indeed — it was a considerable adult pastime in a great many countries.

Hot Cockles was a popular party game in the blindfold group. One player was blindfolded and had to kneel down with his head on a cushion as if he were about to be executed. One by one the other players came up and gave him a slap. If the victim could correctly guess the name of the person who had hit him they had to change places. A version of the game, which involves guessing who is pulling one's hair, is played in Australia. Why the name Hot Cockles was given to this game is not known.

Brother I'm Bobbed was a popular pastime at Victorian parties with both children and adults. Two people were and the other who did not. These two sat on chairs back-to-back with a blanket over their heads so they could not see. The person who knew the game quietly, and unknown to the other, slipped the blanket from his head so that he could see and hit himself on the head with a slipper at the same time calling out, 'Brother I'm bobbed'. The other player, still under the blanket, is told to enquire, 'Brother, who bobbed you?' The first player then names someone in the party as if he were making a guess. The one under the blanket then receives a slap on the head with the slipper from his partner and the 'Brother I'm bobbed' sequence starts over again, much to the amusement of all the party. This version is, of course, intended to get laughs and can be demonstrated only once. However, it can also be played 'straight' in much the same way as Hot Cockles.

The hitting-on-the-head part of Brother I'm Bobbed is involved in that other party game which delights in the name of Are You There Moriarty? In this the two blindfolded contestants lie face down on the floor with their heads about a foot apart, and attempt to hit each other with a rolled-up newspaper, calling out, 'Are you there Moriarty?' before each strike, scoring a point when a hit is made. The game ends when a previously agreed number of points are scored.

Of the many blindfold games, the author's personal favourite is the Sussex game of Scats. It is a game that requires rural surroundings with a fair number of trees within easy reach. The trees are given numbers which everyone must remember. One of the players is blindfolded and stands at a vantage-point. All the others make off and stand behind different trees. The blindfolded player then has to guess which trees hide which players. This game has the elements of Hide and Seek and other 'hunting' games, and it would be interesting to know its period of origin — something, alas, that researches have failed to disclose.

The child's game of Jack, Jack, Show the Light seems to have been inspired by and based on the Jingling Match, although in this case nobody was blindfolded. It is an old game which was played in the dark with tinder boxes in the 17th century. At Eton and Harrow in the 18th century it was known as Hunt the Dark Lanthorn, or Jack-o'Lantern. The player with the light had to show it when instructed to do so, but he could move round to any extent he wished. The other players, of course, had to seek and catch him.

In his book *Cider with Rosie*, Laurie Lee describes a Somerset game called Fox and Hounds which, like Jack, Jack, Show the Light, and its several variations, is played at night. In this the pursuers call out, 'Whistle and holla, or we'll not follo'', and the quarry has to reply.

It is not difficult to detect elements of primitive hunting instincts as well as some elements of simulated punishment and, perhaps, fertility rituals, suggesting possible origins in the distant past.

Recommended Reading

Addison, W. *English Fairs and Markets* (1953)
Alcock, C. W. *Association Game* (1894)
  Cricket (1882)
  Swimming (1894)
d'Allemagne *Sports et Jeux* (1904)
Altham, H. S. and E. W. Swanton *A History of Cricket* (1962)
Anderson, G. *Art of Skating* (1850)
Ashley-Cooper, F. S. *Hambledon Cricket Chronicle 1772-1796* (1923)
Atkinson, Samuel *Ackworth Games and the Men who Made Them*

Baillie, Robert *Letters and Journals* (1638)
Bancroft *Games for the Playground* (1909)
Barclay *Book of Cub Games* (1919)
Batchelor, Denzil *The English Inn* (1963)
Baxter, Peter *Football in Perthshire*
Bazancourt, Baron de *Les Secrets de l'Epee*
Beckford *Thoughts on Hunting* (1899)
Bee *Lives of the Boxers* (1811)
Bernoni, G. *Giochi Populari Veneziani* (1874)
Berry, C. *Portrait of Cornwall* (1963)
Bettesworth *The Walkers of Southgate* (1900)
Blain, D. P. *Encyclopedia of Rural Sports* (1870)
Blaine *Rural Sports*
Blount *Tenures of Land and Customs of Manors*
Bohme *Deutsches Kinderspiel* (1897)
Bohn *Handbook of Games* (1884)
Bolle *Knochelspiel der Alten* (1886)
Bouillet *Acandenie des Jeux*
Bovill, E. O. *English Country Life 1780-1830*
Box, C. *English Game of Cricket* (1877)

Cassell's *Book of Indoor Amusements, Card Games and Fireside Fun*
Cassell's *Book of Sports and Pastimes*
Castle, Egerton *Schools and Masters of Fence* (1892)
Christian, Roy *The Country Life Book of Old English Customs* (1966)
Clark *A Royal and Ancient Game* (1899)
Collins, W. L. *Public Schools* (1867)
Cook, Rupert Croft *Darts* (1936)
Corbett, Martin *Swimming* (1890)
Cotton, Charles *The Compleat Gamester* (1674 and 1680)
Coxwell *My Life and Balloon Experiences*

Cranford, Caroline *Folk Games* (1908)
Crowther and Ruhl *Rowing and Track Athletics* (1905)

Daft, R. *Kings of Cricket* (1893)
Daniel *Rural Sports*
Day, J. Wentworth *Inns of Sport* (1949)
Dingley *Touchers and Rubs* (1893)
Dixon *Gladiator to Persimmon* (1901)
Douglas, Norman *London Street Games* (1916)
Dowling *Fistiana* (1864)
Drabble, P. *Staffordshire* (1948)

Egan *Boxiana* (1818 and 1824)

'Fairfax' *Complete Sportsman or a Gentleman's Recreation* (1763)
Felix *On the Bat* (1845)
Felton W. *New Guide to the Town of Ludlow* (1822)
Finn, Timothy *Watney Book of Pub Games* (1966)
Fletcher, J. S. *History of the St Leger* 1776-1901
Ford *Theory and Practice of Archery* (1887)
Fosbank, Thomas *Dictionary of Antiquities*
Fouquieres, Becq de *Les Jeux des Anciens* (1869)

Gibson, Henry *Tobogganing on Crooked Runs* (1887)
Godfrey *Treatise on the Useful Art of Self Defence* (1740)
Goodman, N. & G. A. *Handbook of Fen Skating* (1882)
Gomme, Alice *Traditional Games of England, Scotland and Ireland* (1894-95)
Grace, W. G. *Cricketing Reminiscences*
Greener, W. W. *The Breechloader and How to Use It* (1899)
Griffin, H. H. *Athletics* (1891)
Gutsmuths, J. C. F. *Spiele fur die Jugend* (1796)

Handelmann, H. *Volks- und Kinder-Spiele aus Schleswig Holstein* (1874)
Hansard *Book of Archery* (1840)
Hargrove *Anecdotes of Archery* (1845)
Headland, I. T. *The Chinese Boy an Girl* (1901)
Hennings *Fights for the Championship* (1902)

Hole, Christina *Custom and Usage* (1941)
English Sports and Pastimes (1948)
Homer *Iliad*
Hone, William *The Every-Day Book* (1825 and 1827)
Table Book (1827)
Year Book (1832)
Howlet, Robert *The Royal Pastime of Cocking* (1709)
Huff, Darrell *How to Take a Chance* (1959)
Hutchinson *British Golf Links* (1897)
Husenbeth *The History of Sedgley Park School* (1856)
Hutton, Alfred *The Sword and the Centuries* (1901)

Inouye, J. *Wrestlers and Wrestling in Japan* (1895)
Irwing, R.L.G. *The Romance of Mountaineering*

Jamieson *Scottish Dictionary* (1808)
Jenkins *Gymnastics* (1890)
Johnson, Mrs T. Fielding *Glimpses of Ancient Leicester* (1906)

Kear, Rev John *History of Curling* (1890)
Kelly, William *Notices Illustrative of Drama and Other Popular Amusements at Leicester* (1865)

MacGregor, Robert *Pastimes and Players* (1851)
McIntosh, P.C. *Sport in Society*
MacLaren *Physical Education* (1895)
Mannix, Danial O. *Those About to Die* (1967)
Markham *Art of Archerie* (1634)
'Marksman' *The Dead Shot* (1895)
Marshall, Julian and J.A. Tait *Tennis, Rackets and Fives* (1890)
Marshall, Rev. P. *Football, The Rugby Game* (1892)
Maspons y Labros, F. *Jochs de la Infancia* (1874)
Miles *Handbook of Boxing* (1838)
Mitchell *Manual of Bowl Playing* (1864)
Mitchell, W. *Billiards* (1897)
Moss, Peter *Sports and Pastimes Through the Ages*
Muncey, R.W.L. *Old English Fairs* (1936)
Murray and Hunter *Physical Education and Health*

Needham, Lt Col Hon H. *Croquet* (1900)

Oldham, J.B. *History of Shrewsbury School*
Oman *Art of War in the Middle Ages* (1898)

Park *Game of Golf* (1896)
Parville, de *La Nature* (1884)

Peesch, Reinhard *Das Berliner Kinderspiel der Geganwart* (1957)
'Philopugilist' *Life of Tom Sayers* (1864)
Piggott, Stuart *Prehistoric India*
Pradeene, A. Vayson de *Prehistory*
Porter, H. *Boston 1800-1835*
Pycroft, Rev J. *Cricket Field* (1887)

Reymond *Alte und Neue Wurfelspiele* (1888)
Rich and Bentley *A New Book of Sports* (1885)
Roberts *English Bowmen* (1801)
Robertson, B.F. *Rugby Football* (1896)
Robinson and Gilpin *Wrestling and Wrestlers* (1893)
Rochholz *Kinderspiel aus der Schweiz* (1857)
Rolland *Jeux de l'Enfance* (1883)
Rothe *Das Kegelspiel* (1879)

Schmidt and Miles *The Training of the Body* (1901)
Scott, Sir Walter *Essays on Chivalry*
Ivanhoe
Scrope, William *The Art of Deerstalking* (1838)
Seymour *Physical Education. Its Theory and Practices* (1898)
Shearman, M *Athletics and Football* (1887)
Shearman, M. and J.E. Vincent *Football. The History for Five Centuries* (1855)
Shufung Yui *Chinese Children at Play* (1939)
Silver, George *Paradoxe of Defence* (1599)
Simpson *Art of Golf* (1892)
Smith *Games and Games Leadership* (1938)
Smith, Charles F. *Games and Recreational Methods* (1926)
Spencer *The Great Game* (1900)
Stephens *American Yachting*
'Stonehenge' *British Rural Sports*
Stowe, J. *Survey of London* (1631)
Strutt, Joseph *Sports and Pastimes of the People of England* (1801)
Suffolk and Berkshire, Earl of Hedley Peek and F.G. Aflalo *The Encyclopedia of Sport* (1897)

Thomas *The Shooting Guide* (1816)
Thompson, James *History of Leicester* (1849)
Thornhill *Shooting Directory* (1804)
Thorsby, John *History of Leicester* (1791)
Timbs, John *Clubs and Club Life in London*
Trotter *Boxing* (1893)

Vassall, Harry *Rugby Game* (1889)
Vignaux *Le Billiards* (1895)

Watson, Alfred *The Turf* (1898)
Webb, Arthur *The Clean Sweep*
White, E. *Practical Treatise on the Game of Billiards* (1807)
Whyte *History of the British Turf* (1840)
Wilton, Lord *Sports and Pursuits of the English* (1868)

Index

Illustrations are indicated by numbers in italics

144